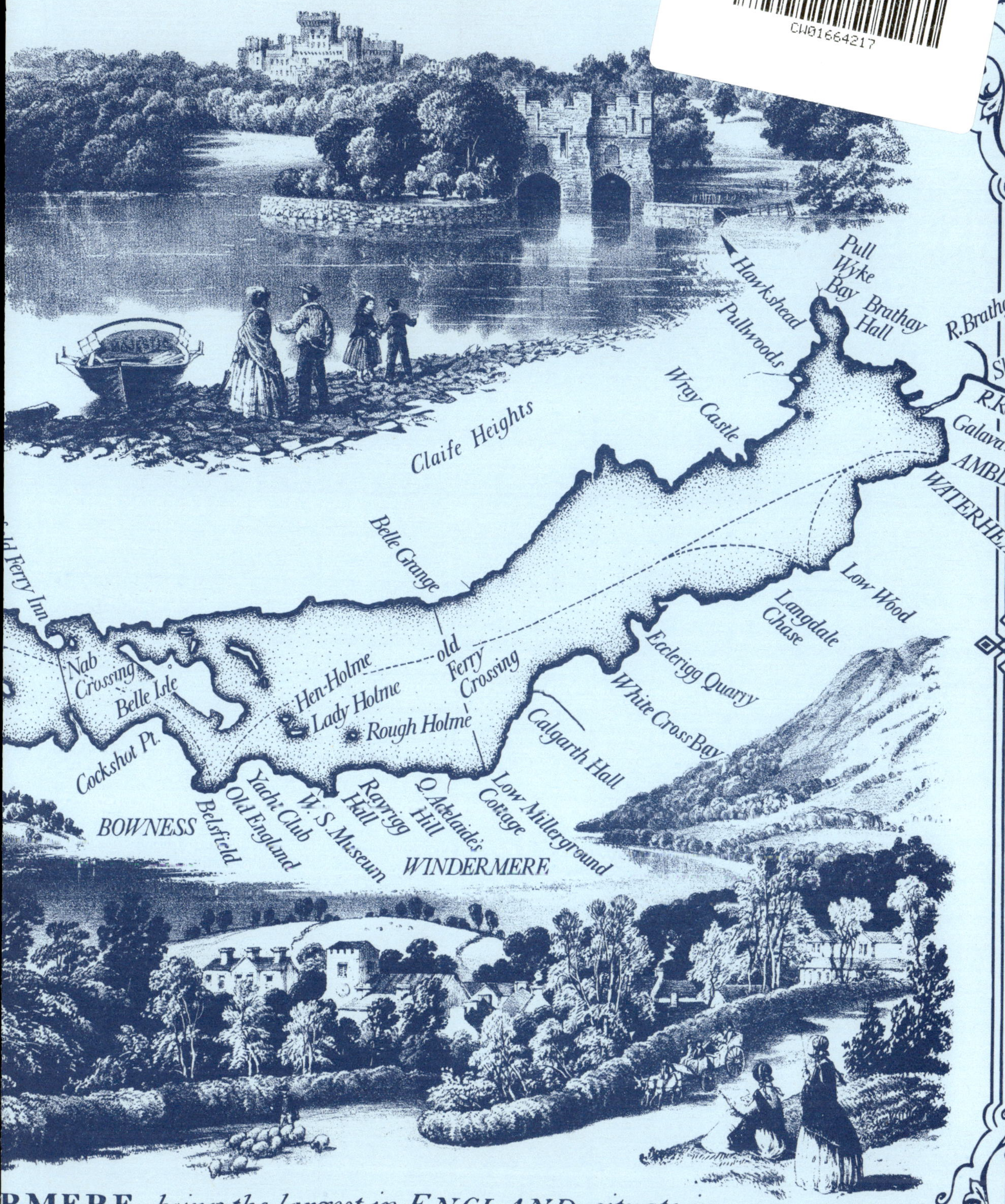

RMERE, *being the largest in* **ENGLAND**, *situate in*
nd LANCASHIRE

The Great Age of Steam on Windermere

BUCKINGHAM PALACE.

It is fortunate for the rest of us that collecting and, if necessary, restoring every kind of thing attracts such dedicated enthusiasts. But for the author's fascination for the steam boats of Windermere the pleasure of seeing his superb collection of what is a delightful blend of art and marine engineering, would have been lost, probably, for ever.

Quite apart from telling the story of the museum, George Pattinson's book is a mine of information about the colourful history of Windermere and the people who have used its waters for fishing, transport and pleasure.

Philip

1981

The Great Age of Steam on Windermere

by George H. Pattinson

George H Pattinson 28th Oct 1988

Foreword by
H.R.H. The Duke of Edinburgh K.G., K.T.

THE WINDERMERE NAUTICAL TRUST
1981

To my wife

Printed in England by Titus Wilson & Son Ltd., Kendal.

Author's Preface

Few lakes in the world have held so much charm and appeal to so many different people over the generations as Lake Windermere. Its story is however unique, in that the march of history culminated in the nineteenth century with a great age of steam and a display of splendour and grandeur the like of which will probably never be seen again. This era established a tradition amongst boat owners and designers which led to the production of perhaps the finest variety of inland craft ever seen together.

It has been one of my life's interests to collect and preserve the best of these boats and to gather together the various threads making up Windermere's rich and colourful history. This interest was first kindled as a small boy during the happy hours spent messing about in boats, and whilst watching and visiting some of the magnificent yachts, steam launches, and speedboats that filled my schoolboy mind with fascination and excitement. It is not often that one has the privilege of seeing one's most cherished hobby develop into a major enterprise, but the founding of the Windermere Nautical Trust and the opening of the Windermere Steamboat Museum in 1977 by H.R.H. The Prince of Wales was, I hope, a major landmark in the preservation of all that is best in Windermere's history and tradition. The museum was established not only because of the scientific importance of its collection. Two programmes on BBC television, 'Collector's World' and 'Look Stranger', elicited a tremendous response from the public who were overwhelmed with the elegance of the steam launches and the serene graceful age that they represented. It was clear that there needed to be a museum on Windermere to enable people to experience and learn more of the golden age of the lake.

The story will continue, but it is my hope that within the pages of this book and the walls of the Windermere Steamboat Museum, many will discover more of the pleasures of Windermere and its past.

George H. Pattinson

Raaes Wyke
Windermere
1981

Acknowledgements

I am most grateful to my family and friends who have given me so much assistance in the production of this book, and I am indebted to many for their help in supplying information and photographs.

Much of the material was handed down to me by my father and grandfather, and the fascinating way they spoke about the life of Windermere during the 19th century provided the inspiration for this book.

I also make grateful acknowledgement to the following for the use of their photographs: Abbot Hall Art Gallery 66, Viscount Boyd 93, High Wray, Village Hall Management Committee 66, Rolls-Royce Limited 81, Raymond Sankey 35, 42, 43, Olive Wilson 70, Barry Smith 70, Storrs Hall Hotel 17, Mrs. B. L. Thompson 6, 67.

Contents

Foreword	page ii
Author's Preface	v
Acknowledgements	vi
Contents	vii
List of Illustrations	viii
Chapter 1 **Oar and Sail**	12
Chapter 2 **The Arrival of Steam**	23
Chapter 3 **The Public Steamers**	34
Chapter 4 **Private Steam**	45
Chapter 5 **Salvage and Restoration**	56
Index	102
Bibliography	103

List of Illustrations

	page
Windermere regatta	2
Char netting	5
Oar ferry	6
Ferry Inn	7
Millerground ferry landing	8
Windermere regatta	10
Lady of the Lake launch	12
Lady of the Lake poster	14
John Bolton bookplate	16
John Bolton	17
Storrs Temple	18
Rayrigg Hall	21
Waterhead Bay *c.* 1850	22
Lady of the Lake bow	23
Old Oliver Haddock	24
Dragonfly	26
Lady of the Lake & *Lord of the Isles*	29
Dragonfly and timber yard	30
Rothay	33
Swift	34
Bateson's Band	35
Swan	36
Swan aground	37
Raven and *Waterhen*	38
Raven with *Barge Elizabeth* & *Iris*	39
1871 steam ferry	40
Ferry with Furness Abbey coach	41
Teal	42
Swift's crew	43
Tern	44
Building of *Swift*	45
Charles Fildes' *Fairy Queen*	46
Dolly in Ferry House Bay	48
Col. Ridehalgh's *Fairy Queen*	49
Linnet	50
Mr. Bowler's steam launch	51
The Belsfield	52
Esperance	53
H. W. Schneider	54
Rowing party	55
20ft. class yachts	56
22ft. class yachts	57

	page
Dodo	58
Britannia	59
Iris	60
Britannia firing a salute	62
Tea party on *Britannia*	63
A. R. Sladen	64
Bat	65
Phantom	66
Powerful & *Mary Anne*	67
Sand barges	68
Wind	69
17ft. class yacht	70
Otto	71
Branksome	72
Elfin, bow on	73
Elfin, beam on	74
Kaiser Wilhelm II on *Maru*	75
Satanella	76
Wagtail	77
Waterhen	78
Canfly	80
SST airship	81
Rolls Royce Hawk engine	81
Sir Henry Segrave	82
Miss England II	83
Peggy	83
Home Guard patrol	84
Home Guard gunners	85
Shorts Sunderland flying boat	85
Modified Falcon I glider	86
Modified Falcon I glider in flight	86
1780 and 1745 *Yachts*	87
Lady Elizabeth	88
1899 motorboat	89
H.R.H. Prince Philip on board *Branksome*	90
Dolly as a wreck	91
Dolly after restoration	92
H.R.H. The Prince of Wales on *Branksome*	93
Windermere Steamboat Museum	94
Swallow	95

Chapter 1

One of the great Windermere regattas from an engraving by Pyne, *c.* 1820.

Oar and Sail

Since the beginning of civilization, the waters of Lake Windermere have formed a focal point for the activities of those who have lived on her shores. They have been used for transport and fishing, and more recently for leisure pastimes such as yachting and steam boating. In this century the motor boat has broken the peace of oar, sail and steam.

Long before the age of steam, the Romans used Lake Windermere for transporting men and supplies. In about AD70 they established precarious control over the hill folk, known as Brigantes, who had lived in the area for some 200 years. At Waterhead they built the strategically placed Fort Galava, one side of which was bounded by the lake and another by the River Brathay. The fort was on the tenth Antonine itinerary, a Roman road, which led from Watercrook near Kendal to the important port of Ravenglass, which was used for trading with Ireland. The road also linked a line of forts through the Lakes, designed to keep the local population in subjection.

Galava was a wonderful vantage point from which the Romans could command a view of the strategic routes over the High Street range of mountains to Brougham near Penrith, and over Wrynose Pass to the magnificently situated fort at Hardknott, which stood out as a bastion of Roman domination high on the desolate fells. Even today one cannot fail to be impressed, when one sees the Romans' engineering capabilities and imagines them protecting their important highway by maintaining a day-to-day military presence in this isolated spot. Galava was first constructed in wood by Agricola in AD69, but it was later strengthened and re-built in stone in AD122. When Hadrian reorganised the defences to his wall at about this time, the Romans probably had a stone quay at Galava, and possibly another toward the south end of the lake near Fell Foot. There may also have been a villa on Belle Isle, which was presumably used by the commander of Fort Galava. Evidence of this, in the form of pavements, pottery and household utensils, was discovered when the foundations of the present house were built in the mid-eighteenth century.

Despite their military and administrative strength, the Romans were unable to retain control over the Brigantes once problems in Rome began to multiply. They gradually withdrew their forces, leaving behind the remains of their forts and roads as a perpetual monument to their former glory. It is very likely that the craft which they had used on the lake were also abandoned, and there may well be Roman vessels buried beneath the silted lake bed awaiting discovery. Whilst continuing efforts are made to locate such wrecks, the depth of the lake and the accumulations of mud make this an extremely difficult task, even when using the most sophisticated modern equipment.

In about AD 1000 the Vikings invaded the North West of England, probably sailing in longboats from Ireland, where they had previously settled, to Morecambe Bay and other parts of the west coast. Some hauled their boats overland, launched them on Windermere, and established settlements around the lake. The Viking invasion left a lasting contribution to the culture of the region and many place names derive their origin from the Norse language. Local tradition has it that a Viking, called Raae, settled on the lake shore by Rayrigg Wyke (the bay just north of the Windermere Steamboat Museum), and he may well have built his home on the site now occupied by Rayrigg Hall.

The broad local dialect that could be heard in Windermere and the surrounding area at the turn of the century, and particularly the farming terminology, bore a marked similarity to modern Norwegian. The writer's grandfather discovered this for himself, when he visited the Bratlandsdal district of Norway at the turn of the century, and found that he could make himself understood. It is also interesting that the Herdwick, the local breed of sheep, was introduced by the Vikings.

Whilst the reasonably peaceful Irish-Viking settlement was taking place in the North-West, a very different, widesweeping and violent invasion by the Normans occurred in the South. Following the Battle of Hastings in 1066 the Normans slowly extended their power, and by about 1150 Cumberland and Westmorland were part of Norman-ruled England. By 1272 it appears that Walter de Lynsay, a Norman lord, had taken possession of Belle Isle.

Monastic influence was also spreading during this period, and in the thirteenth century the monks of Furness Abbey controlled much of the land between Lakes Coniston and Windermere. The monks built a chapel on the island of Lady Holme, sometimes known as St. Mary's Holme. The use of the chapel continued after the Dissolution of the monasteries and possibly until the end of the sixteenth century. It seems to have been run by two monks who had fishing rights in the lake; rights which were important, as fish would have formed a substantial part of their diet. The two monks appear to have been allowed one boat for fetching timber, and one with ten nets for fishing. By 1570 the lake was divided into three "Cubbles" (upper, middle and lower), the ownership of which was attached to the three largest estates around the lake, namely Rayrigg, Storrs and Calgarth. The owner of a Cubble was entitled to exploit the fishing, boating and ferrying rights in his part of the lake, and in these early days a boat was often sold together with the right to use a specified number of nets.

Char netting on Windermere, a profitable pursuit banned in 1924.

The stone tables, possibly of medieval origin, on the adjoining island of Hen Holme (also known as Table Island) may have been placed there by the monks. The tables definitely existed in the seventeenth century, as they bear an inscription that Christopher Phillipson, who lived at Rayrigg Hall, was there in 1605 and 1631. It is thought that he used the island as a retreat, going there on Sundays after Morning Service and remaining until evening.

The first recorded references to the lake relate to the early ferry service. By mid-medieval times Kendal and Hawkshead were wool trading centres of some importance, and the lake formed an obstacle between the two towns which had to be overcome. The principal crossing, now known as the Nab crossing, was over the narrowest part of the lake, just below Bowness, where today's ferry now operates. The first mention of this early ferry is in 1454, and it is referred to again in various documents in 1574. However it is renowned for the great tragedy of 19th October 1635, when a party was returning from a wedding at Hawkshead. It is chronicled by Hoggarth of Troutbeck that:-

> the great boat upon Windermere water sunck about sunsetting when was drowned fforty-seaven persons and eleaven horses. From suden death libera nos . . . .

The victims were buried at the east end of Bowness Church in a mass grave, and one can imagine the lasting effect that this profoundly shocking event had on the local community.

Traditional oar ferry at the Nab crossing in 1853. This was part of the main road from Kendal to Hawkshead.

An early photograph of the Ferry Inn and Windermere row ferry.

Other ferries are also known to have existed, although there is very little information about them. One, probably a small boat, crossed from Millerground on the east shore, to Belle Grange on the west, but it is not known how long this service continued. Certainly there is no record of it after 1600. From the middle of the seventeenth century the ferry rights at the Nab crossing were owned by the Braithwaite family of Braithwaite Fold, but they then passed to another branch of the family in 1707. With the rights went the responsibility for the maintenance and safety of the boats, which had to be tarred once a year. The old ferry bell, which used to hang in the belfry at Low Millerground Cottage and was used for calling the ferryman, is still in existence. Another small ferry may have run from Belman Landing near Storrs. The ferryboat, which can be seen on the lake in front of the old inn in the photograph on this page, is believed to have been built in 1799 and to have sunk in the lake.

One of the ferry landing points on the east shore showing the belfry used to summon the ferryman.

The design of the row ferries changed little over the centuries, with stern ramps and long sweeps, similar to those of *Mary Anne* which is preserved today (see plate). In 1870 the regular row service at Nab crossing was replaced by a chain ferry, which wound its way across the lake using steam power. Often the horses had to be taken out of their shafts, and the carriages or carts, never more than two or three on one ferry, were manhandled down the ramp into the boat. The horses were usually placed with their heads facing the centre to prevent them from jumping overboard. Amidships was a plank resting on the gunwales, on which the oarsmen sat and manipulated the long sweeps. The oars were fitted with upright wooden pegs, attached to the upper part of the oar shaft and grasped by the rowers. Sometimes the passengers assisted the ferrymen and in windy weather some strength and skill must have been required to hold course across the lake. The whole procedure would have taken considerably longer than the present ferry and would certainly have tried the patience of the modern motorist. The cries of the coachmen and carters would ring out across the valley, as they used to call for the boat long before they reached the Nab crossing to try to save time.

Certainly by 1836 and probably before, the wherries of Gibson of Ambleside and White of Newby Bridge were plying the length of the lake. These boats, which were sometimes assisted by sail, were timed to connect with the coach service from Newby Bridge to Lancaster and Ulverston. One boat left Ambleside for the Ferry Nab crossing, where it met the boat from Newby Bridge, and they each then returned to their respective bases. The full journey took three and a half hours and cost three shillings (15p); the trip to the ferry cost one shilling and sixpence ($7\frac{1}{2}$p). Two new boats, built by William Watson of Ambleside, were launched for Gibson and White in May 1844, and were added to the service, but with the advent of the first public steamer in 1845, the wherries were no longer competitive and were discontinued.

There is evidence that, towards the end of the eighteenth century, the lake was used for purposes other than food, trade and transport, as there were regattas for both sailing and rowing boats. Not a great deal is known about the use of the lake for recreation before this period, but in 1796 Captain Quale sailed his yacht, *Peggy*, to Greenodd from the Isle of Man, and then transported it overland to Windermere, where he competed in races with John Christian Curwen of Belle Isle. There is strong evidence to suggest that the boat used by Mr. Curwen was built in 1780 at Workington, although its name has never been discovered.

Later there appear to have been regular regattas based on the old Ferry Inn, one of the earliest being in 1818. The regattas were lively and entertaining with races for both rowing and sailing boats, and as

The splendours of oar and sail at one of the Windermere regattas, captured on an engraving by Pyne.

many as sixty to ninety boats attended. In addition, there were often wrestling bouts and sports on the green behind the inn. It is reported that in 1857 Charles Dickens and his friend, Wilkie Collins, attended one great regatta and Dickens even tried a "fall" with Thomas Longmire, a champion wrestler from Bowness. These contests were the predecessors of the Grasmere Sports and gradually ceased as the Grasmere Sports became more and more popular.

The lake was not only a barrier which had to be crossed and the central point for leisure activities; it also provided the easiest method of transporting heavy cargoes. Although mainly used on Lake Coniston, a good example of the type of barge used for this purpose was *Elizabeth*, now at the Windermere Steamboat Museum. She was built at Waterhead, probably by Mr. Watson in about 1830, and taken to Coniston, where she was used to carry copper ore. At first she would have been rowed, but later she may have been towed by an early steamboat. During the 1880s she was brought back to Windermere with a team of twenty horses and used as a sand-barge.

On Windermere, the barges were used for taking slate down the lake from the wharf at the confluence of the rivers Rothay and Brathay. The wharf was known as "Three foot Brandreth", a reference possibly to the depth limit for barge traffic. Stone was also transported from places such as Ecclerigg quarry and used in building around the lake. The quarry, with its large smooth faces of rock, is interesting on account of the many inscriptions which were carved in the early part of the nineteenth century. The impact of the forthcoming age is highlighted by one engraving, which stands out amongst the many references to the national heroes and burning political questions of the day – carved in large letters on a stone 8 foot square is the legend "STEAM".

Launch of the *Lady of the Lake* in 1845, the first public steamer built for any lake in England.

Chapter 2

The Arrival of Steam

In 1845 the famous iron steamship, *Great Britain*, sailed from Liverpool to New York in just fourteen days. This was a major landmark in the history of steam, but on Windermere an event took place, which must have assumed equal, if not greater, importance in the minds of the local inhabitants. On Saturday 31st May 1845 the *Lady of the Lake* was launched.

Commissioned by Mr. J. B. Fell of the Windermere Steam Yacht Company, and built by Richard Ashburner, a Greenodd shipwright, the *Lady of the Lake* weighed forty-nine tons. Although she was 75 feet long and 11 feet 6 inches in the beam, she drew only 16 inches of water. It had originally been intended that she should be screw-propelled, but it was found that paddles were required to enable her to negotiate the shallow waters of the River Leven down to Newby Bridge. The paddle boxes were made as small and insignificant as possible to avoid spoiling her fine lines. Her engines developed twenty horsepower giving a maximum speed of 9 m.p.h.

The launch took place at Newby Bridge, and was a grand and festive occasion. The Ulverston Brass Band was invited and tents were erected for visitors. Bright flags fluttered from the steamer, from trees and buildings, and from yachts moored on the river. Two boats, loaded with Mr. Fell's guests, attended the ceremony. Having first taken a trip to Blakeholme, they landed on the quay, and Mr. Fell instructed Mr. Ashburner to make the final preparations for the launch. The traditional bottle of champagne was then broken against the vessel's wooden hull, and the first steamer ever to sail on an English lake glided gracefully into

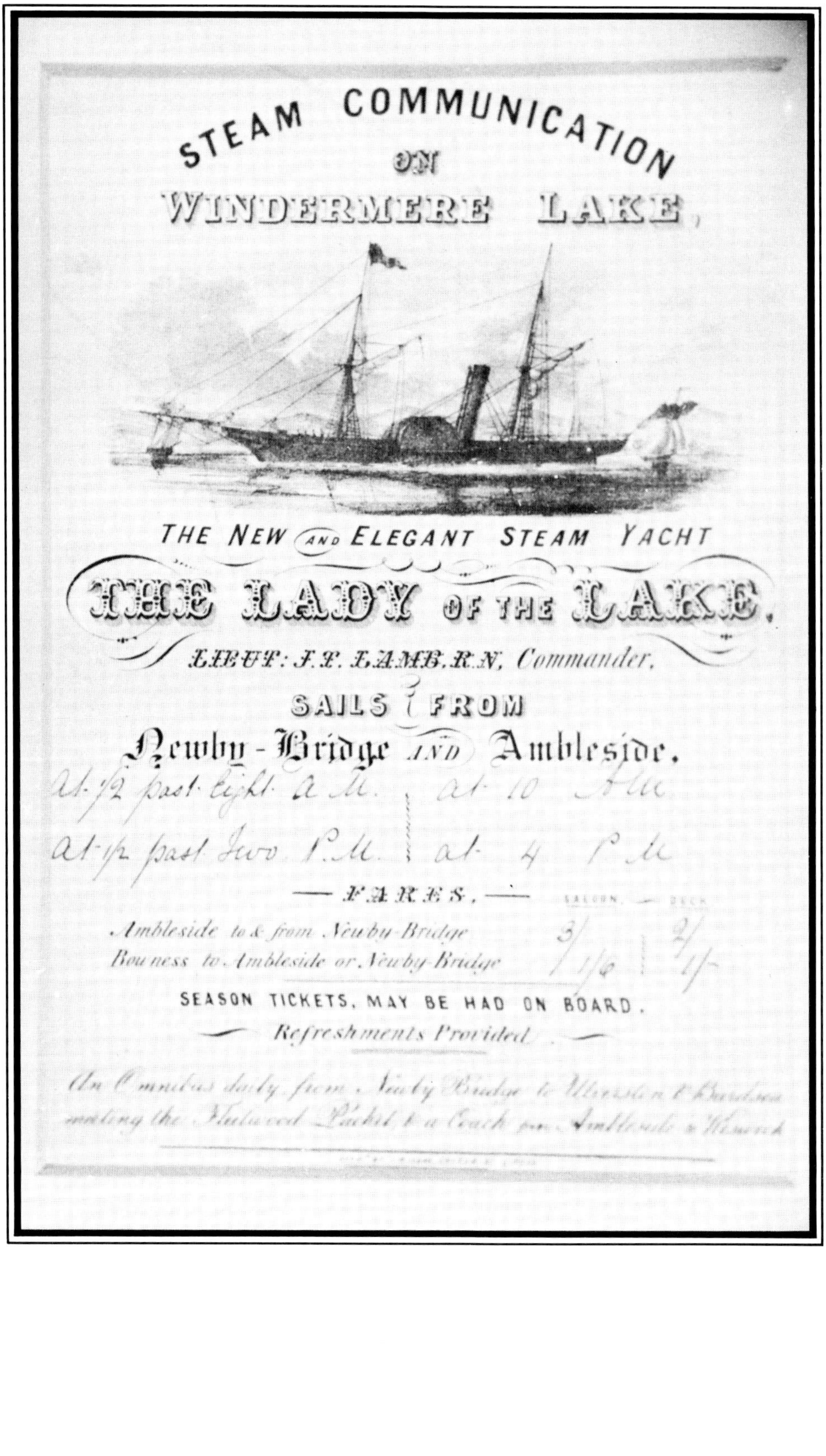

Poster proclaiming the service offered by the *Lady of the Lake* in 1845.

the water. The band played and the spectators cheered heartily. A pennant displaying the boat's name was then unfurled and drew forth another loud cheer for the *Lady of the Lake*.

One can well imagine the beauty of this first lake steamer. She was schooner-rigged with a tall funnel, flanked by masts and rigging, and had a long bowsprit. Her black hull, with gilded moulding and a well-worked figurehead of the Lady of the Lake in white, must have been very striking. Inside, the saloon was luxuriously decorated in pink and white, with handsome carpets and mirrors.

After the launch a dinner took place in honour of the occasion. John Wakefield of Kendal presided and in addition to Mr. Fell's guests, there were about 50 carpenters, who had worked on the *Lady*, and who were accompanied by their friends.

By 26th July 1845 the fitting-out of the *Lady of the Lake* was complete, and steam was raised for the first excursion up the lake. After a luncheon and the appropriate speeches, Mr. J. B. Fell presented an inscribed silver snuff box to Richard Ashburner, as a mark of satisfaction with his work. The *Lady of the Lake* steamed up the River Leven and out on to Lake Windermere for the first time, her paddles churning the water to a white froth, and her tall thin funnel emitting black smoke. Despite her shallow draught, a certain amount of dredging had had to be carried out in the river; the large boulders which were pulled out, using horses and chains, still mark one of the former fords today. After her maiden voyage, the *Lady* returned to the foot of the lake and the party of visitors danced on deck to the music of the Kendal Cavalry Band. On the following day, the programme was repeated for another party of local gentry and friends, but this time to the strains of the Kendal Yeomanry Band. Regular public services commenced immediately, twice a day at first, and once a day in the winter.

Although it seems almost inconceivable today, the coming of the *Lady of the Lake* aroused mixed feelings. The new service was popular with tourists, but was publicly denounced by some members of the local community. The Reverend Charles Mackay records that:-

> the inhabitants . . . of Bowness, Low Wood, Ambleside and generally the gentry of the neighbourhood set their faces against it and would not use it . . . even for the conveyance of a parcel – so annoyed were they that their darling lake should be disturbed by the revolution of the paddle, or their clear atmosphere contaminated by the smoke of a funnel.

However, as the *Lady of the Lake* emerged for the first time on to a lake, which had seen only oars and sail, one wonders whether the local population truly realised the magnitude of this new venture and the new

Plate bearing testament to the grandeur of John Bolton's estate and incorporating symbols of his cultural and trading interests.

era which it heralded – a new era, which was to see not only rapid development in the field of transport, but also far reaching changes in the social and economic structure of the district. One can imagine the calm tranquility of the lake in those early days before tourism became established. Her shores would have been thickly wooded, with very few houses, and as the *Lady of the Lake* steamed north she would pass Fell Foot on the east shore, the great mansion of Mr. Astley. Later this was to be the residence of Colonel G. J. M. Ridehalgh, who purchased the premises in 1859 and built a splendid neo-gothic dockyard, where he subsequently kept two of the largest private steamers on the lake, The *Fairy Queen* and *Britannia*.

Proceeding up the lake past Town End to the east, and Silverholme to the west, she would reach Storrs Hall on her right. This was one of the principal residences on the lake, the property of the late Colonel John Bolton, and in 1845 occupied by his widow. One of the great patrons of the early regattas, Colonel Bolton, a Liverpool ship owner amassed his fortune trafficking in slavery. His involvement in this grotesque trade resulted indirectly in a curse being placed upon him and his house. His business took him all over the world and it is said that he formed a chain of romantic attachments in each of his ports of call. On one fateful

John Bolton, the great slave trader, patriot and owner of Storrs Hall.

occasion when leaving port, one of his ladyfriends swam out behind his pinnace and pleaded to be allowed to join him on the voyage. However Colonel Bolton was deaf to her entreaties and in a fit of rage he drew his sword and severed her fingers at the knuckle as she grasped the gunwale of his boat. As the unfortunate girl sank back with a shriek she cursed him and his house forever. As fate would have it, Colonel Bolton did indeed die without issue, and for generations Storrs Hall was always regarded as an unhappy house.

This gruesome tale apart, it should be remembered that slavery was not universally recognised as being abhorrent at that time, and indeed Bolton proved himself the most patriotic of Englishmen during the Napoleonic Wars, when he raised a fighting force of several hundred men which he paid for out of his own pocket. He was also responsible for one of the most notable regattas ever held on the lake when he entertained Sir Walter Scott, Christopher North, William Wordsworth and the future Prime Minister, George Canning at Storrs Hall. Later the house was owned by the Colonel's nephew, the Reverend Thomas Staniforth, an Oxford Blue, who stroked the first boat to row against Cambridge, its oarsmen donned in top hats for the occasion. Towards the end of the nineteenth century Storrs Hall became an hotel.

Storrs Temple, built in 1804 to commemorate Admirals Howe, Nelson, St. Vincent and Duncan, near Storrs Hall.

At Storrs, the *Lady* would steam past a beautiful little temple on a causeway jutting out into the lake. This was built in 1804 to honour Nelson and his admirals, and was known as the Temple of Heroes. Yacht races sometimes took place from the Temple, and later it was from an adjoining pier that passengers from Storrs Hotel hailed the public steamers by means of a signal, not unlike those formerly used on the railways.

As the *Lady* churned north, she would see the picturesque old Ferry Inn, with Claife heights towering above. Then she would head towards the largest island on the lake, Belle Isle. For many years, Belle Isle, known then as Longholm, was owned by a branch of the Philipson family. During the Civil War, Major Philipson, nicknamed Robin the Devil, successfully resisted a siege by Colonel Briggs and his Roundheads for eight days. Eventually his brother, who had been on the King's business in Carlisle, came to his rescue. The next Sunday, Robin the Devil rode to Kendal in search of Colonel Briggs. Learning that he was at Church, Robin rode his horse straight up the aisle, intending to kill his enemy on the spot. Unfortunately Robin had been misinformed, and as he hastily swung his horse around before the altar and ducked outside, pursued by an irate congregation, his helmet was knocked off. The helmet can still be seen hanging over the Church door to this day.

Agnes Strickland, in her diary written in 1649, mentioned a house of Gothic design flanked by four towers on Belle Isle. Some sources suggest that this house was demolished in 1777, but this seems to conflict with the Machell Manuscript of 1692, which contains a sketch of the Philipson's White Hall that does not accord with Agnes Strickland's description. The present Round House was built by Mr. English in 1774, but it was left to Isabella Curwen to complete the estate, when she acquired it in 1778.

Turning into Bowness Bay, the *Lady* would berth near a few houses clustered around the old Church, including the Georgian residence of Colonel Elms, which stood on the site of the present Old England Hotel. Slightly above the pier was the great new residence of Belsfield, which was being built for the Baroness de Sternberg.

On leaving the small jetty at Bowness and going out on to the upper reaches of the lake, the steamer would have passed the small islands of Hen Holme and Lady Holme, where the old chapel once stood, and would see Rayrigg Hall to the east. This was the residence of the Reverend Fletcher Fleming, who had entertained Queen Adelaide, widow of William IV, five years previously. Queen Adelaide was rowed up the lake on 24th July 1840 and climbed a small hill behind Rayrigg Hall, known then as Rayrigg Bank and now called Queen Adelaide's Hill. There are few better views than the one from this hill, even likened by Christopher North to the Hanging Gardens of Babylon. It is said that after she had climbed the hill, Queen Adelaide retired to Rayrigg Hall to take tea, and as she sat down she is alleged to have exclaimed, "thank God for that", being quite exhausted after her steep ascent. The trip up the lake was in Mrs. Bolton's grand cedar barge, which was quite magnificent, with four oars and oarsmen, and a fine Chippendale chair for the Queen under the awning aft. Unfortunately the boat was taken to pieces and made into rowing boats by Mr. Brockbank of Windermere after the death of the Reverend Staniforth in 1887.

On several occasions William Wilberforce came to Rayrigg to rest from the rigours of London political life. His final visit in 1788 left a lasting impression, for he recorded:-

> I never enjoyed the country more than during this visit, when in the early morning I used to row out alone and find an oratory under one of its wooded islands in the middle of the lake . . . .

It is ironic that whilst Rayrigg Hall housed the draftsman of Britain's anti-slavery laws, Storrs Hall, just three miles down the lake, was later to be the home of the wealthy slave trader Colonel Bolton.

Rayrigg Hall where William Wilberforce drafted some of his anti-slavery legislation.

Artist's impression of Waterhead Bay around 1850 with the *Lady of the Lake*.

A rare photograph of the *Lady of the Lake* showing the renowned figurehead of the lady on her bow.

After passing Rayrigg, the ferryman's little cottage with its belfry at Millerground would have come into view, from whence in days gone by the ferryman had taken passengers for Hawkshead across to Belle Grange. A little further on, the *Lady of the Lake* would have come to Calgarth Old Hall on the eastern shore, occupied in the early days by the Philipsons. This fine old house is overshadowed by the "Legend of the Skulls". The Philipsons wanted to buy the Cooks' farm a little higher up the road. When the Cooks would not sell, they were invited to dinner at Calgarth and, whilst they feasted, Philipsons' silver was secreted in their coat pockets. The sheriff was then tipped off, and as the Cooks returned home they were apprehended on the highway. The Cooks were convicted of stealing the silver and hanged, but in the courtroom Dorothy Cook laid a curse on Myles Philipson saying:-

> Thou mayest think that thou has managed grandly but that thy plot of ground is the dearest a Philipson has ever bought. Neither you nor your breed will ever prosper, the side you take will lose, all your schemes will fail, and the day will come when no Philipson will own an acre of land and while Calgarth walls stand we will haunt it day and night.

Certainly part of this curse came true, because the Philipson line came to an end in 1714 for lack of male issue and, although the Cooks' farm passed into Philipson ownership, it is reputed that their skulls still haunt Calgarth Old Hall as an eerie reminder of the Philipson's treachery.

As the *Lady* steamed up the lake, Wray Castle would have been seen on the west shore. Newly-completed at this time, it had taken some seven years to build for Dr. John Dawson. The estate had a fine wet dock and a harbour in similar medieval style, where the 20 ton yacht, *Hebe*, was later to be kept.

Old Oliver Haddock, one of the redoubtable boatmen on the *Lord of the Isles* in the early 1850s.

Before entering Waterhead Bay, the *Lady of the Lake* would pass the Georgian residence of Brathay Hall, occupied at the beginning of the nineteenth century by the chronicler and artist, John Harden, whose work gives an intimate and colourful picture of his times. Indeed, there is an interesting reference to the *Lady of the Lake* in one of John Harden's letters, which recounts her first appearance in the upper reaches of Windermere:-

> A. and I were in the wherry and went round to call on Mr. Swinburn and heard of the Windermere steamer being afloat and that she had been up to Waterhead, Ambleside that a.m. and we were curious to find and see her. We found her moored in Low Wood Bay and a large party eating their dinner on board in the cabin. We sailed round and admired her, proceeded and called at Calgarth. They were all away from home, save Mr. Swinburn, he was on the lake. Just as we reached the point of Craams Bay (now known as Calgarth Bay) the steamer, no smoke (self-consuming engine) came running in, dropped anchor and Mr. Swinburn sailing after her. Here he and I greeted each other. We went on board (by invitation) the *Lady of the Lake* steamer and were much welcomed by Cornelius Nicholson, Mr. Fell of Ulverston, Mr. Bryans of Belfield, a Director of the Windermere Steam Yacht Company, the Company which owned the *Lady of the Lake*, and three proprietors of the steamboat and here we lunched enjoying two hours up and down from Wray to Storrs Bay and the ferry — most lovely and agreeable – a pretty and handsome vessel – 2 engines 20 horse power and runs from Newby Bridge to Waterhead in three quarters of an hour. Two trips to and fro daily. No eyesore rather an ornamental object. Novel. The wherry we attached to the stern of the vessel following us and on getting on board were promised to be put out at Waterhead, but, alas, the last of her was to be at Storrs Bay, so poor A. and I had to row two hours hard work – from 4-6. We got home, the ladies wondering but being not apprehensive at our long absence.

Finally, the *Lady* would steam grandly into Waterhead Bay, which had few buildings in those days, and tie up at the small wooden pier, which served the old town of Ambleside. Despite John Harden's reference to a journey of three quarters of an hour, with a top speed of 9 m.p.h. it must have taken the *Lady of the Lake* at least an hour and a quarter to cover the eleven mile journey. The prices were the same as for the passage boats from Ambleside – three shillings (15p) for the full journey and one and sixpence ($7\frac{1}{2}$p) to the ferry.

Thus steam had arrived on Windermere. Despite the local opposition, the passage boats owned by Gibson and White, which took some three and a half hours for the same journey, soon stopped running in the face of the unequal competition. So successful was the *Lady of the Lake*'s first short season, with 5,000 passengers being carried, the Windermere Steam Yacht Company resolved in October to order another paddle steamer, to be ready as early as possible the next year. Soon the railways would be extended to Windermere and Newby Bridge, and tourists would flock to the area in their thousands, bringing about a fundamental change in the social character and economy of the area. Steam had come to stay.

Dragonfly 1850, a double-ended iron public steamer built to rival the *Lady of the Lake*.

Chapter 3

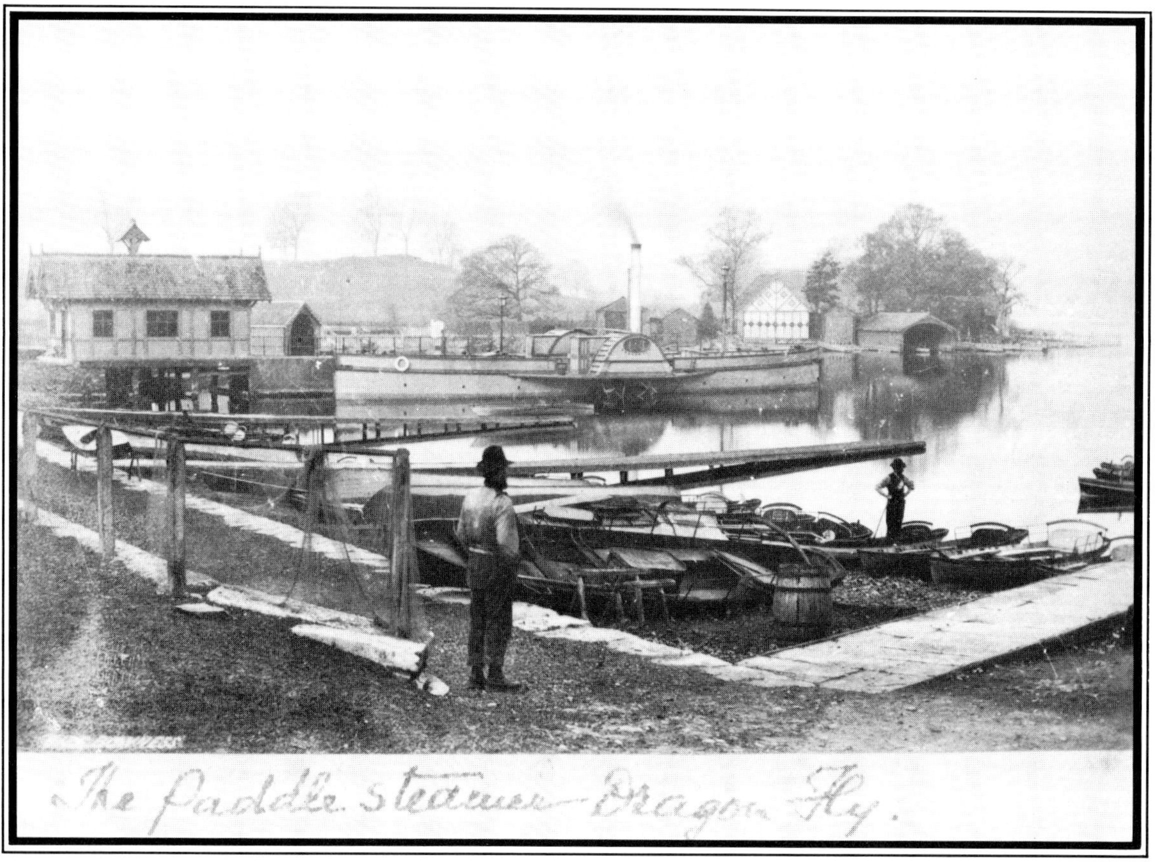

The Public Steamers

On 29th April 1846, just over a year after the *Lady of the Lake* first made her appearance, the *Lord of the Isles* was launched at Newby Bridge. In 1847 the railway to Windermere was completed, and the number of tourists visiting the area increased dramatically.

In their first two seasons, the *Lady of the Lake* and the *Lord of the Isles* effectively dispensed with all competition and established a monopoly in the passenger market. However this state of affairs was short-lived, because a new rival company was formed called "The Windermere Iron Steam Boat Company", which commissioned MacConnochie & Claude of Liverpool to build a paddle steamer with an iron hull. The vessel was built in sections, which were then transported to the new railhead at Windermere and down to Hollbeck Point at Low Wood, where they were assembled on the edge of the lake. The boat's construction must have taken longer than expected, as a paragraph appeared in a local newspaper in March 1849, stating that a new iron paddle steamer would be afloat in the course of a month or six weeks. It would be manned by half the hands required for the *Lord* and *Lady*, consume only a quarter of the quantity of coal, and steam at 12 m.p.h. easily. However it was not until August 1849 that *Fire Fly* was launched, and even then the occasion was not without incident. It had been announced that the new vessel would be launched at one o'clock, with steam up, so that she could make her maiden voyage immediately. Unfortunately the blacksmith was still working on her at the appointed time, and the fire could not be lit. In the event *Fire Fly* was launched late in the afternoon, and did not raise steam until nine o'clock in the evening, when she took a short run towards the ferry. Seventy-five feet long and 11 feet 6 inches in the beam, her dimensions were identical to the *Lady of the Lake*, but on her first test she was reckoned capable of a speed of 12 m.p.h.

Even when launched *Fire Fly* had to be fitted out, and her scheduled services which were announced in July, and again in August, had to be delayed. Once operational *Fire Fly* was soon in trouble. During September, a Kendal newspaper printed letters from indignant correspondents, who had been stranded because the *Fire Fly* had gone off on private afternoon excursions instead of keeping to her time-table. In October 1849 the enterprising directors of the new company set about improving their tarnished image, and *Fire Fly* gave a treat to the pupils of the various schools around the lake. They had three days' play and beautiful weather, and the children excitedly cheered loud and long as they passed the lakeside homes of Mr. F. D. P. Astley and Captain White, these gentlemen being directors of the Iron Steam Boat Company who were responsible for their outing. *Fire Fly* ended the season on 20th October 1849, and the *Lady of the Lake* finished eight days later.

The *Fire Fly*'s first season had not been particularly auspicious, but on 6th February 1850 the Windermere Iron Steam Boat Company resolved to order a further iron boat from MacConnachie & Claude. The new boat was to be christened the *British Queen*, and it was planned that she would run in conjunction with the *Fire Fly* and accommodate two hundred and fifty passengers. Undeterred by previous experience, the company set an impossibly short timetable. The launch was fixed for May, but it in fact occurred ten months late in April 1851, by which time the steamer was known as *Dragon Fly*.

The delay in the building of *Dragon Fly* must have been all the more galling for her owners, bearing in mind the aggressive competition which developed on the lake during the summer of 1850. In July of that year the *Fire Fly*, which had previously sailed at different times from the *Lady of the Lake*, altered her schedule so as to coincide. Strong and bitter opposition grew between the two companies. On the piers pandemonium broke out as stewards, skippers and busmen scrambled to acquire passengers, crying "This way for Ambleside" and "This way for Newby Bridge", amidst the roar of steam and clouds of smoke which emanated from the steamers as they prepared to cast off. On the lake the competing vessels manoeuvred to hinder each other as much as possible. Within eleven days of the change of time-table, on 15th July 1850, the inevitable occurred, and *Fire Fly* and the *Lady of the Lake* collided, although fortunately very little damage was caused.

In August 1850 a disaster overtook the *Lord of the Isles*. Whilst secured for the night at Bowness Steamer Pier, she caught fire and "sustained so

Lady of the Lake and burnt-out wreck of the *Lord of the Isles* in Bowness Bay *c.* 1855.

much damage that it is doubtful whether she will ever be fit to ply on the lake again". Immediate suspicion fell on the fireboys of the *Lord* and the *Lady*, who were charged with wilfully setting fire to the steamer. After preliminary examination at Kendal before a bench of magistrates, the youths were committed to Appleby Gaol to await their trial at the Assizes. In March 1851 Hiley (fireboy of the *Lord*) and Archer (fireboy of the *Lady*) came before Mr. Baron Platt. The evidence was that Hiley had tried to cover himself earlier in the day, by claiming that there was a fire which subsequently proved to be non-existent. The prosecution suggested that this was sufficient circumstantial proof of the boys' guilt, but the judge dismissed the case, saying that it was purely unsupported suspicion and that he believed it most unlikely that the boys would fire themselves out of employment. It is perhaps surprising that nobody appears to have given any thought, as to whether a more likely culprit would not have been some over-enthusiastic employee of the Iron Steam Boat Company.

In September *Fire Fly* had a further accident. After she had landed some passengers at Belle Grange and was proceeding down the lake, her master, Captain Mattix, discovered that one of her plates had stoved in and that she was taking water very fast. With great presence of mind, he ran *Fire Fly* aground opposite Low Wood Inn before the passengers realised what had happened. The men working on *Dragon Fly* at Low Wood were called to repair the damage, presumably delaying the launch of *Dragon Fly* yet further.

In 1851 *Dragon Fly* at last joined *Fire Fly*, having had several experimental trips during April, before being delivered to her owners. She was elegantly fitted and considerably larger than *Fire Fly*, being 95 feet long and 16 feet 6 inches in the beam. Rivalry was still fierce and, although she was still more expensive than the *Lady of the Lake*, *Fire Fly*'s fares were lowered. The Iron Steam Boat Company also offered free trips by rowing boat to Newby Bridge, when the River Leven was too shallow for the steamers, and there were offers of porter brown ale "to warm the cockles of the hearts" of the steamer company's chilly patrons. The *Lady* was slower than her rivals, and *Dragon Fly* used to steam past her with the band playing "The Girl I Left Behind Me".

Dragonfly seen at Bowness Pier with the timber yard in the foreground, 1870.

Three years later in 1854, it was found that the *Lady of the Lake*'s hull had rotted and that she needed re-planking. To do this they used the new dry dock, which had been built at the old Ecclerigg Quarry in 1849. The overhaul was carried out by Messrs. E. J. Schollick of Ulverston, and the *Lady of the Lake* was described as being "greatly improved in speed and beautified in appearance". At the same time, the *Fire Fly* and *Dragon Fly* were undergoing repairs and repainting in preparation for the new season.

Not long after this the *Lady of the Lake* again seems to have had problems. In September 1854 her owners offered a reward of £10 to anyone who could give information as to the whereabouts of some missing machinery. No clue was found, until one day a crewman observed the stolen parts on the lake bed in Bowness Bay. They were salvaged at once, and the *Advertiser* commented:

> From this it would appear that the conjecture at the time formed was somewhat true; the objects of the miscreants being not plunder, but private injury to the Company.

In March 1856 there were great celebrations after the Declaration of Peace, at the end of the Crimean War. Duking Astley, a director of the Iron Steam Boat Company, had a bonfire and a firework display at the edge of the lake. Although out of season, the iron boats were steamed especially and did a roaring trade. By now the initial rivalry had subsided and a calmer and more rational approach prevailed. On 15th May 1856 an advertisement, announcing that the Windermere Steam Packets had commenced their service, was signed "by Order of the Directors of the Windermere Steam Yacht Company and Iron Steam Boat Company". This co-operation was the prelude to the amalgamation of the two companies in April 1858, when they became The Windermere United Steam Yacht Company.

The steamers still occasionally had their difficulties and one accident was of an alarming nature. It occurred in July 1857, when the *Fire Fly*, having left Newby Bridge at 3 p.m., struck some rocks near the centre of the lake opposite Storrs Hall. In those days these well-known rocks would probably not have been marked, and *Fire Fly*'s captain cannot have been very familiar with the lake. The forward part of the boat was badly damaged, and she soon began to fill with water in the fore-cabin. The force of the impact caused the funnel to come crashing down on to the deck, but fortunately there was no injury to any of the passengers. The boat's machinery was not damaged, and in a few minutes the vessel was running again towards the Old Ferry Inn, where the passengers were safely landed.

In 1861 it was the turn of the *Lady of the Lake*. The vessel was crowded with passengers when she was found to be leaking, and there was widespread panic as the cry went up that the ship was sinking. Perhaps remembering the earlier incident with *Fire Fly* at Low Wood, the captain ran the steamer ashore near Belle Grange. Once she was aground there was even greater confusion, as passengers jumped into the water to wade ashore, some of them suffering bad sprains and bruises. Fortunately the steamer returning from Ambleside was alerted to the *Lady*'s plight by the frantic blowing of her steam whistle and the passengers were taken aboard and put ashore at Bowness.

It seems that shortly before the incident, the new United Steam Yacht Company had instigated a winter service. The exact commencement date is not certain, but there was definitely such a service by 1861. This is known because John Love, an Ambleside tailor, obtained judgment against the steamer owners in the County Court for loss of time and expenses incurred by the refusal to take him on board at the Waterhead landing stage. He had wanted to go to Bowness on business, but was the only passenger waiting for the boat. The steamer was already running late and, to save time, ignored his request to stop. One can well imagine his anger at being left stranded on the pier on a cold winter's day, and no doubt he felt vindicated by the judge's award of seven shillings [35p] as damages – not a princely sum, but a timely reminder to the new steamboat company of its duty to the public.

It is not known exactly when the *Lady of the Lake* was withdrawn. There was some suggestion of selling her in about 1863, but it was eventually decided that she should continue to run for another season or two. She had certainly stopped running by 1865, when a more modern vessel was launched. There is a photograph, taken in Bowness Bay in 1870, in which the *Lady of the Lake*'s paddle boxes and funnel can just be seen lying in Mr. Rawlinson's boatyard at Old Fallbarrow.

In December 1865 the Windermere United Steam Yacht Company presented its Annual Report, and it appears that the results of the previous season's operations had been very satisfactory. The directors recommended a final dividend of $12\frac{1}{2}\%$. They stated that they were glad to see that a new iron steam boat had been ordered from the Lancaster Ship Building Company on the basis of a model designed by Douglas Hebson, a naval architect from Liverpool, and that it would be ready to be launched on the lake in time for the next season. "Should the weather next year prove as propitious as it was last year," the report read, "we have no doubt that the Company will be as prosperous as the supported enterprise deserves, and should the contemplated railway scheme meet with no drawbacks, the time will come when the Queen of the Lakes and all the beauties which surround her will be still more thronged, and large steamers will convey the pleasure-seeking crowds over the rippled waves of Windermere."

The new iron steam boat referred to was the *Rothay*, and she was launched in June 1866. In March 1866 the people of Greenodd were surprised by the appearance of a handsome screw steam boat coming up the estuary. Steam vessels seldom visited Greenodd, and this one was probably the largest and finest ever to have been seen. She was the *Duchesss of Lancaster*, an iron boat with an Archimedean screw, and her cargo consisted of materials required for constructing the *Rothay*. The *Duchess of Lancaster* remained at Greenodd for a whole day, and her decks were thronged with visitors, giving a carnival-like atmosphere.

Paddle steamer *Rothay*, an early iron hulled passenger steamer, launched 1866.

Rothay was launched on the River Leven, just north of the Swan Hotel, by the daughter of G. S. Crewdson, a Kendal banker. The new vessel was 105 feet long and 15 feet in the beam, with first and second class cabins. The best of the cabins had seats of polished East India teak, which was also used for the deck fittings. The last public paddle steamer to be launched on Lake Windermere, the *Rothay* had bows at each end and, since the wheel was in the centre of the vessel, she could be sailed up and down the lake without having to be turned in the narrow width of the Leven. After the launching there was a luncheon with speeches, in which humourous references were made to the absence of a chimney, as it had not then been fitted. The guests then made their way to Bowness, entertained by the band of the United Steam Yacht Company. At the end of July the *Rothay* completed her maiden voyage without a hitch, and immediately joined *Dragon Fly* and *Fire Fly* in regular service.

The Directors' Annual Report of 1865 also referred to "the contemplated railway scheme". In November of the same year the Furness Railway Bill was presented to Parliament, providing for the construction of a new branch line, which would extend the Arnside-Ulverston Service to a new pier at Newby Bridge. Under the Bill the Furness Railway Company was given a controlling interest in the Windermere United Steam Yacht

Swift leaving the Lakeside terminus. The station tower was used partly as a lighthouse for winter evenings.

Holidaymakers were entertained by Bateson's Band amid the Palm Court splendour of the Lakeside terminus.

Company. Later the railway company must have extended its plans beyond establishing a railhead down the river, as in 1869 the railway was built as far as Lakeside, where it ended at a grand Victorian terminus.

The buildings were typical of those built by railway companies at the time, with finely wrought ironwork and slender fluted columns. Above the covered pier was a restaurant in the style of a conservatory. Glass skylights and large windows facing the lake and mountains were hung with ferns, and one could await the next steamer in comfort, whilst listening to the sounds of Bateson's Band. At night, a beacon shone from the neo-gothic tower of the terminal building, guiding the steamers to the pier as dusk set in early on winter evenings. It is sad that the original buildings have now nearly all been demolished.

Swan, built in 1869 shortly after the opening of the Lakeside Furness Railway terminus.

The coming of the railway line to Lakeside gave a further boost to tourist traffic, which had already received its first impetus between 1845 and 1847, with the launch of the *Lady of the Lake* and the construction of Windermere Station. Round trips were now offered and holidaymakers could take the train to the south end of Coniston, where they boarded the passenger steamer, *Gondola*, and steamed to Waterhead at the top of Coniston. They were then conveyed by charabanc to Waterhead, Windermere, where a Furness Railway steamer was waiting to take them to Lakeside, from whence they returned home by train.

No doubt having the new development in mind, and aided by the improved access which the railway afforded, the United Steam Yacht Company commissioned the first large screw-propelled passenger vessel, which was built at Lakeside by T. B. Seath and Company of Rutherglen near Glasgow. The new steamer was launched on 1st June 1869 by the daughter of Sir John Ramsden, an eminent Barrow businessman. Weighing seventy-one tons, she was called *Swan* and was 150 feet long and 17 feet in the beam. Colonel G. J. M. Ridehalgh of Fell Foot loaned his steamer, *Fairy Queen*, to assist in the launch, and as *Swan* slid into the water, cannon were fired from the *Fairy Queen*'s deck. One month later when *Swan* had been fitted out, she made her maiden trip to Storrs Hall, and the next day she conveyed a party to Waterhead at the north end of the lake. A particularly fine and fast steamer, *Swan* is reputed to have been capable of 18 m.p.h. – very much faster than *Fire Fly, Dragon Fly* and *Rothay*, which were still sailing in 1869. For many years she had a carving of a swan on her bows, and she remained in service for 68 years. However, those years were not without the occasional mishap, for in November 1893 *Swan* sank at her moorings, and a few years later she sank again, having collided with *Tern*. Her most spectacular disaster occurred in September 1907, when she ran ashore off Belle Grange on a foggy autumn day. She must have been going at a fair speed, as her bow nearly crossed the road, and she had to be jacked up before *Tern* and *Swift* could pull her off.

Swan aground at Belle Grange in 1909. She sank on two occasions before being broken up in 1936.

Raven about her daily deliveries in 1911 with *Waterhen* making the first flight off water.

As in previous times the lake was not only used by tourists. Roads were still poor and apart from the railways, the horse and cart was the fastest mode of conveyance overland. The lake therefore continued to provide the easiest and most efficient method of transporting large cargoes to its remoter parts. Thus the directors of the Furness Railway Company saw an ideal opportunity to combine the new railhead with a steam cargo service. They again commissioned T. B. Seath & Company to build *Raven*. This steam cargo boat, launched in 1871, was to provide essential supplies to the scattered lakeside settlements for many years, and to do for commerce what the *Lady of the Lake* had done for passenger transport twenty-six years previously. It is said that the directors, in determining a name for *Raven*, were influenced by the analogy of the biblical story about the prophet Elijah being fed by ravens in the wilderness.

Flood in Bowness Bay 1898 with *Raven* alongside the pier and early sandwharf, *Barge Elizabeth* and S.L. *Iris*.

Raven was berthed at the north of the Lakeside landing stage, where she was usually loaded on Mondays, Wednesdays and Fridays, for deliveries around the lake on the following days. Her cargo included coal, timber, animal feeding stuffs and barrels of beer. She was also used to transport saltpetre and sulphur for the gun-powder works at Elterwater. A wide range of landing places were used around the lake, but the saltpetre, brought all the way from India, and after 1884 from Chile, had to be unloaded and stored at Pullwyke, where it was kept entirely separate from the Sicilian sulphur discharged at Waterhead. In winter, *Raven* performed an additional service, breaking the ice for the public steamers. This must have been most welcome as in February 1870, before *Raven* came on the scene, the *Westmorland Gazette* reported that the "regular battle between Old King Frost and the Steam Yacht Company, in which the former ultimately proved victorious," had taken place, with one steamer having been stuck in the ice.

Raven also called regularly at High Cunsey, where goods were off-loaded for Hawkshead. The use of Cunsey avoided the steep hill of Briars Brow, which was a difficult obstacle for heavily laden carts coming from the ferry landing at Swines Ness. For many years, botanists were unable to explain the presence of the blue flower, Prickly Borage, which was not native to the district and only grew on the Cunsey landing. Eventually it was discovered that the seed had come with *Raven*'s cargoes of coal from south Lancashire, and had then germinated beside the quay at which the coal was unloaded.

Trips on *Raven* were not always without mishap, for it was apparently the custom to tip the crew with a glass or two of beer once supplies had been delivered. On at least one occasion, a well-rewarded crew member had to be lashed to the small crane amidships to prevent his falling in during the return journey to Lakeside. *Raven* continued in service for many years, but by 1922 she was no longer the major source of contact and the provider that she had once been. The roads had improved and motor vehicles were common, so *Raven* ceased to ply as a cargoship. At the same time the winter passenger service, which was affected by the same factors, was discontinued. The passenger steamers continued to rely on the summer tourist trade, but *Raven* was used by Vickers Armstrong Limited, for testing underwater mine-laying equipment. By the early 1950s she had been abandoned, but her faithful service was to be rewarded with her salvage and restoration in 1956.

A tranquil scene with the 1871 steam ferry leaving the Ferry Nab.

The coming of steam also affected the old row ferry, which had operated at the Ferry Nab crossing for so long. The design and construction of the new steam ferry, which must have been quite a novelty at the time, was supervised by an engineer, George Dixon, of Bella Wray. The boiler and engine were on the same side, causing a list to one side, and barrels had to be lashed to the opposite side to counteract this. Later these were removed, and the ballast was put inside the hull. The ferry's steam engine was used, not to drive paddles or a propeller, but to haul the boat across the lake by means of a chain around a winding wheel. The chain was eventually replaced by a wire rope, but this alone was not entirely satisfactory, as on two occasions it snapped. In one case the ferry drifted on to Rampholme, near Storrs, and the other time it floated as far as Belle Isle; after this an additional guide rope was added for safety.

The Ferry seen in Victorian times with the Furness Abbey coach on board.

The 1870 ferry crossed the lake regularly for forty-four years. In its early days it carried the Coniston coach every day in the summer, and the Hawkshead carrier's cart three times a week. In 1914 it was replaced by a slightly larger boat, which was built at Ferry Nab by workmen brought down from Scotland. These men found it difficult to keep away from the inns at Bowness, and were often absent for two or three days a week until their money had gone. It may have been because of these habits that the boat accidently launched itself. It almost reached Belle Isle before it was arrested and towed back for completion. Once properly commissioned, the new ferry sailed alongside the old ferry for a while, until her owners were satisfied that she was quite safe and not a danger to the public. From 1920 onwards the service was run by Westmorland and Lancashire County Councils. The present motorised ferry, *Drake*, was originally powered by steam when it was introduced in 1954, but it was later converted.

Teal steaming north from Bowness Bay on winter service.

Although the twentieth century and the internal combustion engine brought the age of steam to a gradual close, it continued to play an important part on the lake for many years. Apart from the ferry, *Raven* was in commercial service of one kind or another until 1922 and *Swan*, the passenger steamer of 1869, was in regular service until 1938. The sister ships, *Cygnet* and *Teal*, which were similar but slightly smaller than *Swan*, being 100 feet long and 14 feet in the beam, also plied the lake for many years. They were built and assembled on the Clyde, and once completed, were sailed to Greenodd in 1879, and from there they were transported by rail to Lakeside. This can have been no mean feat, and it is a tribute to the engineering skills of their builders, that the two steamers carried passengers almost without interruption during the summer months, *Cygnet* for 66 years, and for 39 years in the case of *Teal*.

The proud crew of the Windermere Steam Yacht Company on *Swift* at the turn of the century.

Nor were these sister ships the last steamers to be launched. In 1891 the 120 ton *Tern* was built by Forrestt of Wyvenhoe. This vessel replaced the *Rothay* when she was broken up, and could take six hundred and thirty-three passengers. Nine years later in 1900, *Swift* was added to the fleet. One hundred and fifty feet long and 21 feet wide, she was much the largest steamer ever to have been launched on Windermere at that time. With a speed of 15 knots, *Swift* could carry seven hundred and eighty passengers. She was built by T. B. Seath and Company and it is interesting that she cost just £9,500.

In 1936 the new motor vessel *Teal II* was launched, and two years later she was followed by her sister ship, *Swan II*. Each vessel could carry eight hundred passengers, and they were the first steamers on the lake to have bridges placed high above the top deck. In August 1956 Her Majesty Queen Elizabeth II travelled from Ambleside to Bowness in *Teal II*. The grand old ladies of the lake, *Tern* and *Swift*, are still operational today, albeit now under diesel power. With *Teal II* and *Swan II* they carry about seven hundred and fifty thousand passengers a year, an annual turnover one hundred and fifty times greater than the *Lady of the Lake* in her first year.

Built in 1890 and still in use today, *Tern* is one of the fine vessels produced by Forrestt of Wyvenhoe.

Swift being assembled at Lakeside in 1900 for the Furness Railway Company. Note rivet brazier on the right.

One of the great early pioneers, Charles Fildes, with his *Fairy Queen*, c. 1855.

Chapter 4

Private Steam

The public steamers catered for the thousands of tourists, who flocked to the Lake District from all over England. However most of these tourists were only visiting for short periods. The Victorian Age was also one in which the upper classes and the wealthy factory owners prospered, and this section of the community tended to come to Windermere for longer periods, usually buying their own houses on the lake shores. Some of the more adventurous kept their own private steamer in a boathouse at the end of the garden.

Very little is known about these early private steamboats, but first and foremost amongst the enterprising men, who experimented with the new technology, was Charles Fildes, a Manchester businessman with interests in tin plate. In 1850 he built the *Fairy Queen*, the first private paddle steamer recorded as having been used on the lake; we are fortunate to have a photograph of this boat, opposite. Charles Fildes was certainly a steam fanatic, and it is said that he used to take the boiler and engine out of the *Fairy Queen* during the winter and use it to steam a miniature locomotive in the garden at his home in Sawrey. Thus he was able to satisfy his passion for steam when the weather was inclement for lake steaming. Like many of his contemporaries, Mr. Fildes used to go by train to Manchester and in later life it was a familiar sight to see him on his tricycle, making his way to Windermere Station.

Another boat of this period was the steam launch *Dolly*, built in about 1850, and surviving to this day. She can be seen in the photograph taken around 1870, behind the old Ferry Inn, near to Charles Fildes' later

Dolly in Ferry House Bay before her transfer to Ullswater.

steam launch *Cygnet*. *Dolly* was probably owned at this time by Charles' elder brother, Alfred.

There was one early steam launch, built around the same time, which belonged to Mr. Rawlinson. His boat was probably the first iron steam launch on the lake, but unfortunately not even the name of this delightful boat is known. One cannot help but be fascinated by these pioneering days of steam and the early experimental boats with roughly-made boilers and engines. One can imagine too the exciting novelty of stoking up a fire and steaming out on to the lake.

One of the landmarks in private steam was Colonel Ridehalgh's *Fairy Queen*, built in 1859. She was a most elegant craft, measuring 65 feet 10 inches long. Her quite extraordinary journey overland before being launched on the lake is an event worthy of mention. Although there must presumably have been a good reason, it was decided that when she had

The beautiful *Fairy Queen* of 1859, finely appointed – even with gas manufactured on board for lighting.

finished her trials on the Clyde, she would be steamed to Parkhead, near Holker. This was a very strange decision, for the distance between Parkhead and Fell Foot is some ten miles, whereas if she had been taken to Greenodd, she would have had only two miles to travel. Nevertheless the route had been determined, and in April 1860 *Fairy Queen* arrived at Parkhead.

Firstly, the vessel was hauled out of the water and on to the trailer, which had been awaiting her arrival. Then she set off on her journey to Fell Foot, towed by about twenty-five horses. All went well until the convoy arrived at Bigland Scar, where the road had been laid with planks, for fear that the wheels would sink through the road surface into the soft moss beneath. Unluckily one of the planks broke and the wheels sank. The horses were unable to move the wagon that night, but a fresh team was procured for the following day, and they managed to pull the *Fairy Queen* out of the mud. This was not the end of their difficulties, for on arriving at Cark one of the trailer's wheels had to be repaired. After this the journey proceeded by way of Cartmel, Field Broughton, and Staveley Meadows, but again the wagon foundered and the steamer had to be left over the weekend. After a great deal of effort she was finally extricated from the mire, and the *Fairy Queen* eventually arrived at her destination on the ninth day.

Once launched, *Fairy Queen* figured on the lake for some twenty years. For many of those years she was the finest and most prestigious steamer on the lake, and was used by Colonel Ridehalgh for widely differing purposes. Not only did she assist at the launching of the *Swan* in 1869, but she also attended the many splendid regattas and performed ceremonial duties on public occasions. Colonel Ridehalgh used her to transport both himself and his staff around the lake. No doubt his housekeeper and footman would use her to go to Bowness to obtain stores, as this would be so much easier than making the trip by a very rough road with a horse and carriage.

Mr. Bryans of Belfield and family enjoy a leisurely afternoon on board *Linnet*.

Another interesting feature of the *Fairy Queen* is that she was reputed to have been the first ship ever to have been illuminated with gas manufactured on board. The gas was made by passing a current of air through a small box containing a chemical compound; the air current being produced by a new patent hydraulic blower turned by clockwork and a weight. The cost of the apparatus was £15, and the running costs were rather cheaper than for ordinary gas. She must have caused quite a stir, when she steamed brightly lit into Bowness Bay in April 1863 to demonstrate her new light source. Soon after the launch of her successor, *Britannia, Fairy Queen* was sold, and had a number of owners and several home ports, including Cardiff, Liverpool and Edinburgh, before being taken to Crete, where she was seen berthed in 1911. The final end of this beautiful vessel is shrouded in mystery in a distant land, as only befits a fairy queen.

In the 1860s, several small steamers were launched on to the lake. One such was the *Linnet*, owned by Mr. Bryans of Belfield, which had an engine by Plenty & Son of Newbury mounted on the boiler. There were undoubtedly several other similar craft, which were used by their owners for picnicking in quiet bays and steaming peacefully around the lake. The *Cygnet*, a screw steam yacht built by Robert Rodger of Port Glasgow, is known to have been launched on Windermere in May 1870. Records refer to a choir outing in September 1871 on Mr. White's steam yacht *Cygnet*. It is possible that Mr. White hired out his steamer for private parties, and he may have been connected with the Swan Inn at Newby Bridge.

Mr. Bowler's steam launch, typical of many smaller launches which plied the lake in Victorian times.

In February 1869 Henry William Schneider, the Furness industrialist, moved from Oak Lea, Furness, to Belsfield, the 1845 home of the Baroness de Sternberg. Mr. Schneider had made his fortune prospecting for iron, and was largely responsible for the development of the Furness iron industry. He was a great benefactor, and he not only set about improving Belsfield, but brought prosperity to Bowness, erecting houses for his employees and building a working mens' club. In 1870 he even paid for the heightening of the church tower. In the year that he moved to Windermere, he commissioned the 65 foot screw-driven steam yacht *Esperance*. Although *Esperance*'s journey overland could not rival the coming of the *Fairy Queen*, it was nevertheless spectacular. She was brought to Lakeside on a purpose-built railway wagon by the Furness Railway Company in which Mr. Schneider had a substantial interest, the railway track being especially strengthened and re-laid through the centre of the bridges en route.

Esperance was built on the River Clyde by T. B. Seath & Co. Her hull was of the highest grade iron, made by one of Mr. Schneider's companies,

The Belsfield, residence of H. W. Schneider, above Bowness Bay around 1870.

and the riveting was counter-sunk to give a smooth finish on the outside. She had a beautifully panelled saloon and particularly fine lines. Her engine was of a unique design in the form of an inverted "V" twin to accommodate her two propellers. The twin-screw was something of a novelty at the time, and one boatman is said to have commented, when told of this unusual feature, "I suppose she must have a propeller at each end?".

Mr. Schneider used to commute each day to his office in Furness. Every morning he left his residence, preceded down the lawn by his faithful butler, Mr. Pittaway, who carried his master's breakfast on a silver tray. The procession then boarded *Esperance*, where Mr. Schneider ate in the

H. W. Schneider's *Esperance* approaching her pier in Bowness Bay *c.* 1880.

H. W Schneider, the great Barrow iron magnate, M.P., philanthropist and owner of the Belsfield and *Esperance*.

forward saloon, as the vessel steamed sedately to Lakeside. Here he was met by a special train, as there was no scheduled service running sufficiently early for him. His secretary travelled up on the train with the morning mail from Barrow, and he and Mr. Schneider then dealt with the correspondence on the return journey; when coming home the letters dictated on the morning trip were signed. Mr. Schneider adopted this form of travel in all weathers, and the *Esperance* therefore had a reinforced raked stem to deal with light ice.

The pier which Mr. Schneider used for his steamer is still known as the Esperance Pier, in spite of the fact that *Esperance* has not used it for over sixty years. He also used a slipway known as "Lady Slip", which was situated on the south edge of Cockshott Wood. This slipway is thought to have been built for the *Lady of the Lake* in about 1860, when the dry dock at Ecclerigg Quarry proved unsatisfactory.

Esperance remained in Mr. Schneider's ownership until he died in 1887. She then passed into the hands of Mr. Logan, who ran the new Ferry Hotel, which had been built in 1880, and she was used by him to promote custom. On Sundays the yacht ferried Mr. Logan's staff and guests to Wray Church, where they landed at Wray Castle boathouse. Mr. Logan was a keen huntsman, and he kept hounds on Crowholme (or Hound

Holme as it is often known), immediately north of the Ferry Hotel. He often ferried his hounds in *Esperance* to the parts of the lake where he chose to hunt. Colonel Ridehalgh used to do the same, transporting his harrier hounds from their kennels at Fell Foot. Mr. Logan built the present *Esperance* slip and dock at Ferry Nab. Later *Esperance* achieved fame of a different kind, for she formed the basis of Arthur Ransome's description of Captain Flint's houseboat in the famous children's novel, "Swallows and Amazons". In 1941 *Esperance* sank in twenty feet of water near Blakeholme, but was later salvaged.

The early 1870s were splendid and exciting years on the lake. *Swan*, *Rothay* and *Dragon Fly* carried the increasing number of visitors. *Raven* was delivering her regular cargoes, and the new steam ferry crossed backwards and forwards at Ferry Nab. Colonel G. J. M. Ridehalgh's *Fairy Queen* could frequently be seen, dwarfing the many smaller steamers which thronged the lake.

Gentlemen and their ladies enjoy a summer rowing party in Victorian times.

Windermere's famous 20ft. class established in 1867, jockeying for positions at the start of a race.

In addition to the development of steam, the sport of yachting had also progressed. Early races were sponsored by Mr. J. C. Curwen, at the end of the eighteenth century, and included the spectacular contest previously described between the Isle of Man yacht, *Peggy*, and Mr. Curwen's 1780 boat. Subsequent competitions prospered and the great regattas developed, attended by the Baroness de Sternberg, Mr. Swinburn of Calgarth, Dr. Dawson of Wray Castle, Mr. F. D. P. Astley of Fell Foot, and James Bryans of Belfield. However, the sport really received its impetus from Joseph Bridson and Colonel Ridehalgh, who formed the Windermere Sailing Club on 16th January 1860. Colonel Ridehalgh had bought the fine Georgian residence at Fell Foot from Mr. Astley in 1859, and Mr. Bridson rented Waterside Cottage at Bowness Bay in the same year.

Races were organised for boats of all sizes under a system of handicapping. The boats had removable ballast in the form of shot bags, which had to be moved whenever the yachts went about. This must have been extremely hard work for the crews and the practice was abolished in about 1875. Prizes were often awarded by the wealthy owners of houses around the lake, who sometimes stipulated certain conditions. The Reverend Thomas Staniforth for example, insisted that any race which he sponsored had to finish at Storrs Temple, adjoining his home at Storrs

22 ft. class yachts with their 14 ft. bowsprits and $3\frac{1}{2}$ ton lead keels were renowned for their speed.

Hall. Mr. Astley required his race to end at Fell Foot. In those days, the yachts started from a string of mooring buoys on a chain across the ferry line, each boat being secured to a buoy until the starting gun was fired. Moored boats were usually used to mark the courses.

Many sailing boats took part, but probably one of the largest was the 20 ton *Hebe*. She was built at Cowes and was raced successfully, before being brought to Windermere by Mr. Preston, and being kept at Wray Castle, the home of Mr. Preston's relative, Dr. Dawson. The *Hebe* was really too big for Windermere as her draught was too great. She was laid up for some time, but was bought for cruising by Sir William Forwood in 1869. Eventually she was broken up in 1879, although she was found to be quite sound.

Many of the yachting enthusiasts were steamboat owners as well, and when not participating they watched the fun from the comfort of their steamers. One such was William Inman of the Abbey, a successful businessman, who founded the famous Liverpool shipping line of the same name. He was a rather fearful sailor and always had his steamer, *Wyvern*, in attendance whilst he was racing. Joseph Bridson owned a steamer similar to, but smaller than, the *Esperance*, called *Glow Worm*, which he kept on the other side of the Esperance Pier. In addition there was David MacIver, who owned *Wagtail*, launched in 1872, and *Dodo*, a charming 42 foot paddle steamer, built in 1880, in the coach house block at Wanlass Howe, Waterhead.

Dodo 1881, named after the extinct bird, paddle propulsion being long outmoded.

The Windermere Sailing Club prospered under the control of such illustrious sailors, and in 1887, the year of Her Majesty Queen Victoria's Golden Jubilee, a Royal Warrant was granted to the Club. Thereafter it was known as the Royal Windermere Yacht Club. In 1884 a club room was opened in the Old England Hotel, but this proved inadequate as a result of the swiftly increasing membership, and in 1888 the site of the present club house was purchased, adjoining the Old England Hotel.

One of the great occasions on Windermere, was the launch for Colonel G. J. M. Ridehalgh of S.S. *Britannia* at Fell Foot. There can seldom have been a lake vessel built to such magnificent specifications. Modelled on the *Fairy Queen* but very much larger, the steamer was built in sections by T. B. Seath & Co. These were then transported from Rutherglen on the Clyde to Lakeside, where they were assembled during the end of 1878 and the beginning of 1879, before the vessel was launched by Miss Ridehalgh on 24th June 1879.

The symbol of grandeur, *Britannia* provides the setting for many a memorable occasion.

Iris being conveyed on a timber waggon drawn by a Burrell no. 2254. This traction engine is remembered locally for its headlong dive into Thirlmere, its rebuilding and long life in the area.

An iron screw steamer, *Britannia* was schooner rigged with two masts, and had an overall length of 110 feet. Her twenty horsepower engines by Plenty & Son gave a speed of 16 m.p.h. The cabins were exquisitely panelled, and Colonel Ridehalgh ordered special china and cutlery for use on board, decorated with the Ridehalgh family crest and the name of the ship. One of *Britannia*'s saloon hatches, with some of its beautifully painted glass windows almost intact, was found in 1979 in a garden in Barrow, being used as a greenhouse roof. It was donated to the Windermere Steamboat Museum for restoration. Tragically *Britannia*, which was probably the grandest and most opulent vessel ever to grace the waters of Windermere, and which dominated the lake during the last twenty years of the nineteenth century, was broken up in 1916. During her lifetime she was the scene of many celebrated parties, and she epitomised the luxury and extravagance of Victorian high society. One of the most notable occasions was when she attended the celebrations which marked Queen Victoria's Golden Jubilee, and fired a salute from her cannon.

Britannia firing a salute from a miniature cannon on the occasion of Queen Victoria's Golden Jubilee in 1887.

Tea aboard Col. Ridehalgh's *Britannia* after a Royal Windermere Yacht Club race.

The year 1887 marked the end of an era in Windermere, for in July two of the most distinguished men in the district, died, — Mr. H. W. Schneider and the Reverend Thomas Staniforth. Interestingly, they were never good friends, and Mr. Schneider preferred to steer clear of Storrs, when sailing to and from Lakeside in the *Esperance*. With the passing of these two gentlemen began the decline of the large privately maintained country houses around the lake, both Belsfield and Storrs Hall becoming hotels after their owner's deaths.

As one era closed another began, and in the following year the Sladen brothers, Alfred and Mortimer, arrived in the district. Alfred Sladen in particular had an outstanding genius for design and sufficient wealth to enable him to actually put his ideas into practice. Year after year a continuous flow of yachts and steam launches came off his drawing board and were built to his order.

A. R. Sladen, the great all-rounder, yacht and steam launch designer, athlete and helmsman.

Alfred Sladen was an amazing man. In addition to his talent as a boat designer, he was also a brilliant yachtsman and a superb sportsman. In the great frost of 1895, he leaped some fifteen feet across the ferry track on skates – a hazardous enterprise to say the least. In the same winter, he built an ice yacht and covered the distance of one mile between Henholme and the Bark House in just one minute – a speed of 60 m.p.h. Not being content with all this, he could throw a penny over the island of Crowholme from the ferry landing, a distance of about 120 yards. In 1891 Alfred Sladen had the 27 foot steam launch *Bat* constructed, and shortly afterwards his first powerful steam launch the 55 foot *Phantom*. These were to be the first of many steam boats built to Alfred's design.

Bat is renowned for the part she played in some of the first experiments in radio-control, which were carried out in 1904 by two local inventors, Jack Kitchen and Isaac Storey. These two men erected a wireless mast on Queen Adelaide's hill and steered the boat around the north lake, with only a stoker on board to fire the boiler. Much could be said of Jack Kitchen, for his interests were diverse, and his ideas ranged from a gas gramophone to an elliptical wheel designed to facilitate the negotiation of difficult terrain. However three particular inventions are worthy of mention. The first are the Lune Valley boiler and burner, patented by Kitchen and Perkins, which used a paraffin burner and coiled tubes to maximise the heating surface and minimise the water required. As a result, steam could be raised from cold in five to ten minutes. The other device conceived by Kitchen, was the reversing rudder, which dispensed with the need for reversing gear, and was used by the Royal Navy on small boats for many years.

Bat in her heyday, complete with polished brass funnel.

A. R. Sladen's *Phantom* about to disembark the ladies for tea at Wray Castle.

During the 1880s Mr. G. H. Pattinson, the author's grandfather, was one of the first local men to use the lake for both pleasure and commerce. His first steamer, the *Jubilee*, was launched in 1887, but he was to have several others, including the *Wraith* (once owned by Mr. Sladen), which was capable of 17 m.p.h. His vessels, *Powerful* and *Iris*, were used to transport goods and men, around the lake, to various sites which were being developed by his construction business. For example, during the latter years of the nineteenth century the Esplanade development at Waterhead and the buildings at Graythwaite Hall and Pullwoods, were all supplied by these lake steamers rather than by road. When the lake was frozen, as in 1880 and 1895, G. H. Pattinson took advantage of the cold and turned the adverse weather conditions to good account, by arranging for timber on heavily laden wagons to be dragged across the ice by teams of horses. During the First World War rafts of floating timber were towed by *Powerful* from the log shoot south of Bark House to Lakeside. Whenever the steam ferry was out of commission, *Powerful* would be called upon either to tow the old row ferries, or to run a limited passenger service.

Powerful called into service to pull the Windermere Ferry *Mary Anne*.

G. H. Pattinson also developed the commercial dredging of sand from the lake. The original sand wharf was in Bowness Bay immediately to the south of the Railway Company pier, but because the promenade was extended in 1911 and again in 1921, the wharf was moved, slightly further south at first, and then to the site where the Windermere Steamboat Museum now stands. The method of getting the sand was interesting. The sand barges which were towed into position by *Powerful* and *Iris* were about 40-50 feet in length and had a plank down one side. One man stood on the plank with a 12 foot pole, which was fitted with a scoop consisting of an iron ring to which a hessian sack was sewn. The pole was lowered to the lake bed, and another man then pulled it along with the aid of a rope and winch from the opposite end of the barge. A small derrick was used to tip the scoop, filled with sand gravel, into the barge.

However whilst G. H. Pattinson looked to the lake for practical purposes, his wife was renowned for her steamer parties. When the family's own steamer could not accommodate the many guests which Mrs. Pattinson sometimes invited, she hired the *Britannia* and brought the maids from her home at Gossel Ridding to serve the hampers of food.

Sand barges berthed in the dock now occupied by the Windermere Steamboat Museum.

G. H. Pattinson's interests extended beyond steam, for he was also concerned in the development of electric launches on the lake. He was heavily involved with Frederick Fowkes in the development of electric lighting in Bowness and Windermere, and together they built the Troutbeck Bridge electricity works, which in 1893 gave Windermere and Bowness some of the first electric street lighting in Britain. This venture was so successful that G. H. Pattinson built a small hydro-electric generator at Storrs, with a view to providing power to the houses which he was then constructing on the estate. In 1900 he built the dock adjoining Storrs Hall, to house the three prototype electric launches *Shamrock, Rose* and *Thistle.* The launches were powered by banks of batteries, which were stored around the side of each boat, and which were charged by the adjoining generator. One of the launches was always kept on charge. They proved quiet and easy to handle, but the spillage of acid from the batteries unfortunately gave the hulls a very short life.

Wind, one of Windermere's electric launches; sadly the spillage of battery acid tended to shorten the hull life.

Windermere 17ft. class, introduced in 1904 and still raced today. Photograph of W. B. Smith's *Caprice II*.

Otto 1896, one of a generation of steam launches designed and built for speed.

In 1893 Colonel G. J. M. Ridehalgh died. He had contributed so much to the splendour of steam with *Fairy Queen* and *Britannia*, and had played a major part in the development of the Royal Windermere Yacht Club. However, the Club continued to prosper during the 1890s, with new yachts coming off the drawing boards of both Alfred Sladen and Percy Crossley. They were to see the great traditions of the Royal Windermere Yacht Club maintained up to and after the First World War, being involved in the establishment of the unique 17 foot yachts as the premier class. Many of the finest of these boats were built during the 1920s and 1930s and are still raced today.

Alfred Sladen also turned his talents to steam boats and in 1896, designed *Otto* for his brother, Mortimer. One in a succession of high powered steam launches, *Otto* was 43 feet long and 6 feet in the beam and was designed for speeds of 18 m.p.h. or more. Still in working condition, she was constructed by Forrestt and Sons of Wyvenhoe, who specialised in building steel ships, and was fitted with a powerful Sisson's triple expansion engine and a coal fired locomotive boiler. Instead of being riveted, the ship was bolted together, each part being numbered according to a plan and colour coded with painted stripes. Then the newly completed vessel was dismantled, packed and transported to her launching site, where she was reconstructed and riveted together.

It is interesting to compare *Otto*'s sleek streamlining with the elegance and grace of her exact surviving contemporary, the steam launch *Branksome*, which was built for Mrs. Howarth of Langdale Chase by Brockbanks of Windermere. *Branksome* was built of varnished teak, with brass railings and leather seats. The saloon was carpeted and luxuriously furnished with embossed velvet upholstery seats and tasselled fringes. In the galley, she had a solid white marble wash basin with a tap operated by a "beer pump" handle. She was also equipped with heads (w.c.) with a

Branksome 1896, one of the finest steam launches built for Windermere, flagship of the Windermere Steamboat Museum collection.

polished mahogany seat. Another interesting feature was the so-called "Windermere kettle", which enabled one gallon of water to be boiled in 10 seconds. This was a copper urn which contained a coiled steam pipe, through which high pressure steam from the boiler was passed. Many of the steam launches of the period were fitted with this extremely useful device.

Alfred Sladen's most outstanding achievement was his 65 foot steam launch *Elfin*, which was launched in 1895 and was capable of the then quite remarkable speed of 25 m.p.h. *Elfin* developed 240 horsepower, with a high pressure locomotive boiler and an enormous compound steam

A. R. Sladen's *Elfin*, the fastest steam launch built for the lake, approaching her top speed of 25 m.p.h.

The powerful *Elfin*, her slim 65 ft.×6 ft. 6 in. hull enabled her to steam at very high speeds.

engine, the high pressure and low pressure cylinders being respectively 11 inches and 16 inches in diameter with 10 inches stroke. In 1895 Kaiser William II sailed up the lake in Robert MacIver's *Maru*, and *Elfin* carried the Kaiser's staff, greatly impressing the Kaiser with her demonstration of speed.

Queen Victoria's Diamond Jubilee celebrations took place in 1897, and *Elfin* provided the electricity to enable the whole of Bowness Bay to be brightly lit. It is thought that her engine was uncoupled from the shaft and a large generator temporarily installed aft. In the following year during the great flood of November 1898, Alfred Sladen steamed *Elfin* up the River Brathay, and amazingly he was able to reach the lower side of Brathay Bridge and then turn his 65 foot vessel around for the return journey. It is said that when he competed in yacht races, the *Elfin* was made ready by Charlie Astley, who positioned her at the Esperance Pier with her bow pointing outwards, and then awaited his master. Mr. Sladen would roar on to the pier in his car, which would be one of the latest models of the day, board *Elfin*, and steam at full speed to his yacht, which would be waiting with her crew at the starting line. Apparently, he always arrived without fail just before the 5-minute gun.

Kaiser Wilhelm II disembarking from *Maru* during his visit in 1895 escorted by the Earl of Lonsdale with *Dodo*, *Elfin* and *Tern* seen in the background.

It was not long after the advent of *Elfin* that the first motor-boat came on to the lake in 1899. Very little is known about the origin of this early prototype, save that it was built in 1898 and shown at the Paris Exhibition the following year, before being brought to Windermere where it is kept today. It originally had a two stroke engine, which was subsequently converted to a four stroke, and it is interesting that this first design still relied on concepts more appropriate to steam. For example, the cylinder lubrication was drip fed, and the throttle was a valve on the pipe which linked the carburettor to the engine. A variable pitch propeller enabled the boat to be reversed and was worked by hand from a mechanism on the shaft, which pulled the blades over the gears to alter the pitch for forward or astern.

The motor boats and steamers continued side by side for several years, and in the early twentieth century a popular class of Windermere steam boat developed. Two surviving examples of this class are the sister ships, *Osprey* and *Swallow*. *Osprey* was built in 1902, and *Swallow* in 1911, by Shepherd's of Bowness. They were slightly smaller and rather less extravagantly fitted than *Branksome*, being 45 feet 6 inches long and 8 feet in the beam. *Swallow* was powered by a triple expansion engine by W. Sissons of Gloucester similar to, but more sophisticated than, *Branksome*'s compound engine.

Satanella 1907 steaming at 23 m.p.h. and consuming 40 gallons of paraffin per hour.

Another remarkable craft was Williamson's 1907, 38 foot steam launch *Satanella*, which was capable of 23 m.p.h. She had a quadruple expansion engine and a large Lune Valley boiler, which consumed forty gallons of paraffin every hour. The author's father used to tell of carts, loaded with barrels of paraffin, being delivered to *Satanella*'s dock – the cost then was 2½d. per gallon. Tragically, the days of such spectacular craft were short-lived.

It was one of the saddest days in the author's life, when as a young boy in 1926 he boarded the *Elfin* with his father, who had been offered her for just £100. Unhappily, his father made the heart-rending decision not to buy her, and she was scuttled. It has always been the author's dream that one day *Elfin* would be found and restored to her former glory. *Elfin* was not the only steamer to suffer such an ignominious fate, many fine vessels disappeared without trace, and many others were left to rot or were dismantled, their once innovatory design having become outmoded and unfashionable. As steam had eclipsed all forms of competition in the middle nineteenth century, so steam itself was overtaken by the arrival of the internal combustion engine. Times changed rapidly, but happily not everyone was intoxicated with the new noisy and evil-smelling invention. A few preferred to retain the memory of a more peaceful and more elegant age. As a result some steamers survived, and a few more have been recovered before they were lost completely.

David MacIver, M.P.'s elegant *Wagtail* with raked mast and clipper bow.

Chapter 5

Captain E. W. Wakefield's *Waterhen* used for flying instruction.

Salvage and Restoration

During the first years of the twentieth century, the internal combustion engine began to secure its grip over the lake as the great age of steam slowly slipped away. By 1905, a small number of motorboats had joined Mr. Tomlinson's 1898 boat and the Bowness boatbuilders began to lend their skills to the new fashion. More dramatically however, Borwick and Sons in 1910 became involved with A. V. Roe and Co. in the construction of floats for a Curtis-style biplane for Captain E. W. Wakefield, and a hydro monoplane for Mr. Gnosspelius. At first it seemed that the Gnosspelius monoplane would be the first in the air; however, she crashed on take-off, smashing a wing and splintering the airscrew. Although she was rebuilt and flown in 1912, it was Captain Wakefield's *Waterhen* which made the first successful flight in November 1911 and Windermere thus gave birth to the age of the seaplane. The photograph of her flying over the steam cargoboat *Raven* evokes something of the drama of the time and the growing ascendance of the petrol engine over steam.

The early 1920s saw the motorboat become well established and the lure of speed began to entrap the more enterprising of Windermere's boating enthusiasts. In 1924 Major E. H. Pattinson suggested to a friend, Mr. R. B. Stephens, that they form a motor boat club. Later a meeting was held and the Windermere Motor Boat Club was formed on 1st May 1926. Two weeks later a new clubhouse was opened in Bowness Bay, which was to become the centre for a new era of Windermere boating.

Major Pattinson's boat, *Canfly*, epitomised the spirit of experiment and adventure which prevailed after the First World War. Built in 1922, her hull had been especially designed to take a 1917 Rolls Royce Hawk engine, which had powered a Royal Naval Air Service airship, SST3. The boat featured frequently in the Motor Boat Club's early activities, and it is now maintained by the Windermere Steamboat Museum, the engine being acknowledged as the oldest working Rolls Royce aero engine in the world.

In 1930 the lake was to witness the heroic attempt by Sir Henry Segrave in his *Miss England II* to break the world water speed record. The whole country became involved with the build-up to the attempt; the previous

Canfly picks up speed, powered by her 1917 Rolls Royce Hawk aero engine.

An SST airship of World War I with engine housed in gondola suspended beneath.

Rolls Royce Hawk engine similar to that used to power *Canfly*.

Sir Henry Segrave before his epic but fateful attempt on the World Water Speed Record in 1930.

record stood at 92·86 m.p.h. On her first run *Miss England II* reached 96·4 m.p.h. and 101·11 m.p.h. on the second. On the third fateful run she was travelling at nearly 120 m.p.h. when she suddenly spun into the air and crashed, fatally injuring Segrave and his mechanic Halliwell. Following the disaster the wreck of *Miss England II* was miraculously located and recovered from the depth of 180 ft. without the use of divers.

T. C. Pattinson lays a wreath from *Peggy* on the anniversary of the Segrave tragedy.

They succeeded in ingeniously slinging four steel wire ropes between two barges and under the hull of the boat, and winching her to the surface. In spite of the Segrave disaster speed boat racing remained popular, dominated by Borwicks-built boats and "Chris Crafts" of which the Windermere Steamboat Museum's special race boat *Jane* is a notable example.

Miss England II approaching the World Water Speed Record in June 1930.

Between the wars, without the huge number of boat users seen today, it was possible to enjoy the occasional festivity, reminiscent of the great regattas held in Victorian times. Fancy dress parades, bobbing for apples, motorboat and rowing races, swimming and greasy pole fights, provided much pleasure for local people. The author recalls a regatta as a small boy, in which he was dressed up as Noah with a long white beard, and sailed aboard a boat specially converted into a Noah's ark, complete with a selection of animals. In the excitement the hens escaped overboard but happily they were rescued and dried out around the boiler of an accompanying steam launch.

Sadly the gaiety was to be short-lived with the outbreak of the Second World War and once more the lake was almost emptied of boating enthusiasts and tourists. The need to guard the lake against possible enemy flyingboat landings gave the local Home Guard the ideal opportunity to show their mettle, and several pre-war racing boats re-emerged armed with Vickers machine guns. One of their prime responsibilities was the protection of the new Shorts Sunderland Flyingboat Factory at White Cross Bay, where a number of these aircraft were built or repaired for their patrol and anti-submarine role over the Atlantic. The awesome roar of these magnificent four-engined machines as they thundered down the lake became part of the routine on wartime Windermere.

Home Guard afloat and about their duties patrolling the lake.

Home Guard behind a Vickers machine gun, ready and alert for any enemy landing.

Shorts Sunderland flying boat taking off on Windermere ready to join the Battle of the Atlantic.

T. C. Pattinson prepares a modified Falcon glider for its first flight off water in February 1943.

Wartime also gave rise to a project initiated by the War Office and Shorts Brothers to develop a glider to take off water, for dropping behind enemy lines in difficult terrain such as in Norway. A standard Slingsby Falcon I was selected and modified by the author's father T. C. Pattinson, in his company's joiners' shop. On a cold morning in February 1943, the glider sped across the lake behind a speedboat before taking off, soaring over the surrounding hills and successfully landing back on the lake.

The modified Falcon I glider soars over Claife Heights on her maiden flight.

The dark days of war also saw the first significant step in the preservation of Windermere's historic craft. H. W. Schneider's *Esperance* had sunk in 1941 and, Mr. T. C. Pattinson, decided to salvage her. Despite the shortage of tackle, he succeeded in raising the boat in the same manner as the *Miss England II* salvage. Unfortunately, *Esperance*'s two steam engines had been scrapped before the war, but she was carefully restored and is now the oldest boat on Lloyd's Yacht Register. It is hoped one day to re-convert her to steam.

The slow return to normality after the war rekindled thoughts of preserving some of the other historic Windermere craft. However the course of fortune does not always run smoothly as became clear in 1952 when the fine old 1745 yacht preserved in a barn above Rayrigg Bay, was destroyed by fire after small boys had broken in and lit a fire to dry their clothes. The tragedy spurred the author to trace the 1780 Curwen yacht which had been discovered with the 1745 yacht in an abandoned dock in 1934. Armed only with an old photograph and vague rumours, he eventually found the yacht upside down in a field near Southport, in good condition but being used as a hen house. The farmer was more than happy to exchange it for some corrugated iron sheets.

1780 and 1745 *Yachts* being inspected after their discovery in an old boathouse on Windermere in 1934.

The collection slowly began to grow. *Lady Elizabeth c.* 1895 lay sunk in a few feet of water near Cockshott Point, having been abandoned by her owner in 1955. Now powered by a single cylinder engine and a Lune Valley boiler and burner, she is regularly used to troll for char. This local delicacy of the salmon-trout family is usually caught using two rods with ninety foot weighted lines, and with six to eight horizontal lines and spinners leading off. Normally a rowing boat is used to troll, as the lines have to be kept moving continuously to preserve the correct angle. Motor boats are unable to go sufficiently slowly to catch the fish, but *Lady Elizabeth* is ideal and may frequently be seen on the lake on a fine summer evening.

The survival of the 1871 cargo boat *Raven* was a close thing. Having been steamed by the Furness Railway Company, she was left sunk and abandoned and was sold to a shipbreaker in the belief that her useful life was over. The author first heard of this when he was told that the breakers were on board, and rushed to the scene to hurriedly negotiate

The author trolling for char aboard *Lady Elizabeth*.

her purchase. *Raven* was refloated and restored in 1957, and in 1971 her original Campbell's of Glasgow engine was put into working order by engineer cadets of Ocean Fleets Limited. On 18th October 1971 *Raven* celebrated her centenary in steam – a great occasion on one of Windermere's wildest days, with a buffet lunch served below deck in the saloon. Since the opening of the Steamboat Museum, her deck has been completely re-laid and she can now be seen painted in her original Furness Railway Company colours. She is the second oldest vessel in Lloyd's Yacht Register and the oldest with her original machinery.

It was not only steamboats which attracted the author's attention. In 1955 the daughter of Mr. Tomlinson, who used to own the 1898 *Motor Boat* brought to Windermere from the Paris Exhibition, generously gave the boat to the author to restore. The hull had been carefully kept under a hedge and the engine removed and stored in her cellar, thus preserving this important little craft.

The early motorboat brought to Windermere from the Paris Exhibition of 1899.

H.R.H. Prince Philip on board *Branksome* in 1966 with the Admiral of the Royal Naval Sailing Association's flag flying from the bow.

A major milestone in the building of the author's collection was the acquisition of *Branksome*, built in 1896 for Mrs. Howarth of Langdale Chase. The author approached the owner, who was glad to find someone willing to take over the vessel and to restore her to her original condition. At the time the value and historic importance of these craft was not generally appreciated, but interest began to grow a few years later when *Branksome* was used to convey H.R.H. The Duke of Edinburgh down the lake during his official visit in 1966.

On this same occasion Prince Philip also inspected another addition, known then as the "Ullswater Steamer". The salvage of this boat was perhaps the most remarkable of all, as she had been found by divers in Ullswater in forty feet of water. Her clipper bow and the gold line, which still gleamed in the murky water, showed that she was of some interest, although little else could be seen. She was salvaged in 1962, after a carefully planned operation by a team of divers from the Furness Sub Aqua Club, who were led by Gerry Jackson.

When the vessel was raised it was apparent that she was a very early steamer, but nothing could be discovered of her history. She was found to have her original engine and boiler intact, and the author was asked to carry out her restoration. It was an agonising decision whether or not to take on this task, for the salvaged remains looked a sorry and improbable subject for work of this nature, and there was the considerable risk that a great amount of time and money would be wasted if the project failed. Fortunately it was winter and her timber hull dried out slowly, the wood hardened after repeated treatment with preservatives, and no framing of planking had to be replaced. The original spanner was found in the boat and was used to remove the boiler inspection cover. To everbody's astonishment the inside of the boiler appeared to be in good condition, with no rust, scale or pitting of either boiler or tubes. Three years after she was salvaged, on 18th September 1965, the steamer was launched

The wreck of *Dolly* breaks surface with cabin removed but engine and boiler intact, in 1962.

once again. It was a moment which the author will cherish forever, as her simple engine slowly came back to life.

In 1972 a photograph of the boat was discovered, revealing her name, Alfred Fildes' *Dolly*, referred to in Chapter 4. Built in about 1850, she is acknowledged by the Guinness Book of Records to be the oldest working mechanically-propelled vessel afloat. In later life she must have been taken from Windermere to Ullswater, probably over Kirkstone Pass, pulled by either a team of horses or a steam traction engine. Later the exact date of *Dolly*'s sinking came to light. A local man recalled how his grandmother had been awaiting the birth of her baby at an Ullswater cottage. She remembered seeing the *Dolly* afloat in the bay, but after the birth the boat had disappeared. A search through the parish records revealed that *Dolly* had sunk on 21st February 1895, the year of the great frost and had been submerged for sixty-seven years.

By now the author had, almost by accident, acquired a unique collection of historic vessels. Not long after his visit Prince Philip formed The

Dolly steaming on Windermere after her restoration and re-launch in 1965.

H.R.H. The Prince of Wales makes his own tea from the steam urn on board *Branksome* in 1977.

Maritime Trust. One of its members, the late Malcolm Glasier, Managing Director of Ocean Fleets Limited, showed a particular interest in the boats and generously helped to persuade The Maritime Trust to support the building of a museum. After much deliberation and one or two false starts the Windermere Nautical Trust, which had been especially formed to ensure the preservation of the collection, managed to acquire the site of the present museum. Plans were drawn up by the Trust's architect, and in 1976 building of the museum complex began, financed by voluntary contributions and grants from The Maritime Trust and the English Tourist Board.

Many people contributed to the success of the project with their untiring efforts and enthusiasm. These were rewarded when, on a glorious spring afternoon in May 1977, H.R.H. The Prince of Wales opened the Windermere Steamboat Museum as part of the Queen's Silver Jubilee celebrations. In his speech, he referred to the importance of the museum "for preserving ships of this type, without which we would have lost a great part of our heritage". Unlike his great uncle, the former Prince of Wales, who had travelled in the **motor** boat *Beaver* fifty years previously, Prince Charles was taken aboard the **steam** launch *Branksome* and conveyed to the Royal Windermere Yacht Club. On his way he delighted everyone by insisting on making his own tea, using *Branksome*'s Windermere steam kettle.

The museum has enabled the Windermere Nautical Trust to bring together a representative collection of the many varied and historic craft, which have been seen on the lake over the last two hundred years. However, this would never have been possible without the generosity of other enthusiasts. *Bat*, the 1891 launch built for Alfred Sladen, and the 1911 *Swallow*, have been placed on permanent loan by the widow of the late Leslie Goldsmith, who had completely restored both these vessels during his lifetime. *Swallow*'s sister ship, *Osprey*, has been acquired with the assistance of the Science Museum, and has been reconverted to steam for use in giving trips to the public. *Otto*, the 1896 high speed steam launch designed by Alfred Sladen, is kept at the museum by her owner, David Black, and *Water Viper*, a sister ship of *Swallow*, which is loaned to the Trust by J. R. M. Pilling, can also be seen. In 1978 the old row ferry *Mary Anne, c.* 1865, was raised from behind Belle Isle and was donated by Edward Curwen, a descendant of John Christian Curwen who had owned the 1780 boat.

Although the museum was conceived to preserve steam boats and to generate interest in them, the Windermere Nautical Trust has now extended its brief to cover all facets of the usage of the lake. There is now a fine collection of motor boats, including the early motor boat of 1898 and another built in 1903; a Chris Craft Special Race Boat of 1936; and even a 1962 hydro-plane speed boat, *Cookie*, which is already an interesting museum-piece. More humble boats also find their place including an original Rob Roy canoe, built to the same specifications and by the same builder as the canoe belonging to Mr. McGreggor, who made the boat famous with his extensive travels through the northern waterways of Europe in the 1860s and '70s. Also on display is Beatrix

The Windermere Steamboat Museum soon after the royal opening by H.R.H. The Prince of Wales in 1977.

Potter's rowing boat, with a flat bottom so that it could be used on the tarn near her home, and a collapsible canvas coracle that can be carried on the back when hiking. Recently a further departure from the original concept has taken place with the display of the 1943 glider.

Down the ages, Windermere contributed significantly to the maritime history of the nation with her beautiful, unique and fascinating craft. Steam changed the whole character of the lake, transforming it into a bustling tourist centre, and Windermere is now one of the most popular places in the British Isles. Enveloped as it is for many in a romantic aura derived from its natural beauty and the stories from byegone days, the lake presents an enchanting backdrop to the story of steam. It is however, the inventiveness, enthusiasm and enterprise of the early pioneers, and the skill and craftsmanship of their successors that the museum chiefly portrays. These men were infused with the spirit of steam, and it is that spirit which the museum is dedicated to preserve, and which this book has attempted to convey.

Swallow 1911, the classic Windermere steam launch and sister ship of *Osprey* and *Water Viper*.

BIBLIOGRAPHY

Royal Windermere Yacht Club, Atkinson & Pollitt (1906). Edited by Sir William Forwood.

Jones, Sir Clement (1959). *John Bolton of Storrs*, Titus Wilson.

Kipling, Charlotte (1972). *Commercial Fisheries of Windermere*, Cumberland & Westmorland Antiquarian & Archaeological Society (CWAAS).

Marshall, Dr. J. D. (1958). *Furness and the Industrial Revolution*, Barrow-in-Furness Library & Museum Committee.

Melville, J. & Hobbs, J. L. (1951). *Early Railway History in Furness*, CWAAS, Titus Wilson.

Thompson, B. L. (1954), *Professor Wilson of Elleray (Christopher North)*, published privately.

Thompson, B. L. (1971), *The Windermere Ferry: An antiquarian essay*, Titus Wilson.

Wilson, Lord, of High Wray (formerly Lt. Cdr. P. N. Wilson) (1972), *J. G. A. Kitchen, 1869-1940, and his inventions*, Newcomen Society.

INDEX

Abbey, The 58
Adelaide Queen 20, 21
Adelaide, Queen A. Hill 20, 64
Agricola 3
Appleby Gaol 29
Archer 29
Arnside 34
Ashburner, Richard 13, 15
Astley, F. D. L., Duking 16, 28, 31, 56, 57
Astley, Charlie 74
Atlantic 84, 85

Bark House 64, 67
Barrow 37, 54
Bat 64, 94
Bateson's Band 35
Beaver 93
Belfield 50, 51, 56
Bella Wray 41
Belle Grange 7, 23, 30, 32, 37
Belle Isle 4, 9, 20, 41, 42, 94
Belman landing 7
Belsfield 20, 52, 63
Bigland Scar 49
Black, David 94
Blakeholme 55
Bolton, Col. John 16, 17, 21
Bolton, Mrs. 21
Borwick & Sons 79, 83
Bowler, Mr. 51
Bowness Church 6
Braithwaite Family 7
Braithwaite Fold 7
Brandreth 11
Branksome 72, 76, 90, 93
Brathay, river 3, 11, 74
Brathay Hall 25
Bratlandsdal 4
Briars Brow 40
Bridson, Joseph 56, 58
Brigantes 3, 4
Briggs, Col. 20
Britannia 16, 51, 59, 62, 63, 68, 71
BBC Collectors World
BBC Look Stranger
British Queen 28
Brockbank of Windermere 21, 72
Brougham, Penrith 3
Bryans, Mr. 25, 50, 51, 56

Cambridge 17
Calgarth Hall 5, 23, 25, 56
Campbells of Glasgow 89
Canfly 80
Canning, George 17
Cardiff 51
Cark 50
Carlisle 20
Cartmel 50
Charles, Prince of Wales 93
Chile 39
Chris Craft 83, 94
Claife Heights 86
Clyde, river 43, 49, 52, 59
Cockshot Point 88
Cockshot Wood 54
Collins, Wilkie 11
Coniston 5, 11, 36, 42
Cook, Dorothy 23
Cookie 94
Cowes 57
Craams Bay 25
Crete 51
Crewdson, G. S. 34
Crossley, Percy 71
Crowholme 54, 64
Cubbles 5
Cunsey 40
Curwen, Edward S. C. 94
Curwen, Isabella 20
Curwen, John C. 9, 56, 87, 94
Cygnet, Furness Rly 43
Cygnet, Fildes 48
Cygnet 51

de Lynsay, Walter 4
de Sternberg, Baroness 20, 52, 56
Dawson, Dr. John 23, 56, 57
Dickens, Charles 11
Dixon, George 41
Dodo 58
Dolly 47, 90, 91, 92
Dragonfly 26, 28, 30, 34, 37, 55
Drake 42
Duncan Admiral 18

Ecclerigg quarry 11, 31, 54
Edinburgh 51
Edinburgh, The Duke of 90, 93
Edward, Prince of Wales 93
Elfin 73, 74, 76, 77
Elijah 38
Elizabeth II, Queen 44, 93
Elizabeth, barge 11, 39
Elms, Col. 20
Elterwater 39
English, Mr. 20
English Tourist Board 93
Esperance 52-8, 63, 87

Fairy Queen, Fildes 47
Fairy Queen, Ridehalgh 16, 37, 48-52, 55, 59, 71
Falcon I glider 86
Fell Foot 16, 37, 49, 55-9
Fell, J. B. 13
Fell of Ulverston 25
Ferry Hotel 54, 55
Ferry Inn 7, 9, 20, 31, 47
Ferry Nab – see Nab
Field Broughton 50
Fildes, Alfred 48, 92
Fildes, Charles 47, 48
Firefly 27-31, 34, 37
Fleming, Rev. Fletcher 20
Flint, Capt. 55
Forrestt of Wyvenhoe 44, 71
Forwood, Sir William 57
Fowkes, Frederick 69
Furness 52
Furness Abbey 5, 41
Furness Rly 34, 36, 38, 45, 52, 88, 89
Furness Sub Aqua Club 90

Galava 3, 4
Gibson of Ambleside 9, 25
Glasier, Malcolm 93
Glasgow 37, 89
Glider 86, 95
Gloucester 76
Glowworm 58
Guiness Book of Records 92
Gnosspelius 79
Goldsmith, Leslie 94
Gondola 36
Gossel Ridding 68
Grasmere sports 11
Graythwaite Hall 67
Great Britain 13
Greenodd 9, 13, 33, 43, 49

Hadrian 3
Halliwell 82
Harden, John 25
Hardknott 3
Hawkshead 6, 23, 40, 42
Hebe 23, 57
Hebson, Douglas 32
Hen Holme 6, 20, 64
High Cunsey 40
High Street 3
Hiley 29
Hoggarth of Troutbeck 6
Holker 49
Hollbeck Point 27
Home Guard 84, 85
Hound Holme 54
Howarth, Mrs. 72, 90
Howe, Admiral 18

India 39
Inman, William 58
Ireland 3
Iris 39, 67, 68
Isle of Man 9, 56

Jackson, Gerry 90
Jane 83
Jubilee 67
Jubilees Queen Victoria's 59, 62, 74

Kaiser Wilhelm II 74, 75
Kendal 6, 20
Kendal Cavalry Band 15
Kendal Yeomanry Band 15
Kirkstone Pass 92
Kitchen, Jack G. A. 64, 65

Lady Elizabeth 88
Lady Holme 5, 20
Lady of the Lake 12-44, 54
Lady slip 54
Lakeside 34-6, 40, 43, 45, 52-4, 59, 67
Lancashire 40, 42
Lancaster 9
Lancaster Shipbuilding Co. 32
Lancaster, Duchess of 33
Langdale Chase 72, 90
Leven, river 13, 15, 30
Linnet 50, 51
Liverpool 13, 16, 27, 32, 51, 58
Lloyd's Register of Shipping 87, 89
Logan, Mr. 54, 55
Longholm 20
Longmire, Thomas 11
Lord of the Isles 27-9
Love, John 32
Low Millerground Cottage 7
Low Wood 15, 25, 27, 30, 32
Lune Valley Co. 65, 77, 88

MacConnochie & Claude 27, 28
Machell manuscript 20
Mackay, Rev. Charles 15
Manchester 47
McGreggor, Mr. 95
MacIver, David 58, 77
MacIver, Robert 74
Maritime Trust, The 93
Maru 74, 75
Mary Anne 9, 67, 94
Mattix, Capt. 30
Millerground 7, 23
Miss England II 80, 82, 87
Motorboat, 1898 76, 79, 89, 94

Nab, ferry crossing 6, 7, 9, 40, 41, 42, 55
Napoleonic Wars 17
Nelson, Admiral 18, 20
Newbury 51
Newby Bridge 9, 13, 25-31, 34, 51
New York 13
Nicholson, Cornelius 25
Noah 84
North, Christopher (see also Prof. Wilson) 17, 21
Norway 4, 86

Oak Lea 52
Ocean Fleets Ltd. 89, 93
Old Fallbarrow 32
Old England Hotel 20, 59
Old Oliver Haddock 24
Osprey 76, 94
Otto 71, 72, 94
Oxford 17

Paris Exhibition 76, 89
Parkhead 49
Pattinson, G. H. snr. 67-9
Pattinson, Mrs. G. H. 68
Pattinson, Maj. E. H. 79, 80
Pattinson, Capt. T. C. 86, 87
Peggy 9, 56
Perkins 65
Phantom 64, 66
Philip, Prince 90, 93
Philipson, Christopher 6
Philipson, Myles 23
Philipson, Maj. "Robin the Devil" 20
Pilling, J. R. M. 94
Pittaway, Mr. 53
Platt, Baron 29
Plenty & Son 51, 62
Potter, Beatrix 95
Powerful 67, 68
Preston, Mr. 57
Prince of Wales, HRH – see Edward & Charles
Prince Philip – see Edinburgh, Duke of
Pullwoods 67
Pullwyke 39
Pyne, J. B. 2

Quale, Capt. 9
Queen – see Adelaide & Elizabeth II

Raae 4
Rampholme 41
Ramsden, Sir John 37
Ransome, Arthur 55
Rayrigg Hall 4, 5, 6, 20, 21, 23
Rayrigg Wyke 4, 87
Raven 38-40, 43, 55, 79, 88, 89
Ravenglass 3
Rawlinson, Mr. 32, 48
Ridehalgh, Col. G. J. M. 16, 37, 48, 50, 55, 56, 59, 62, 71
Ridehalgh, Miss 59
Rob Roy canoe 94
Rodger, Robert 51
Roe, A. V. & Sons 79
Rolls-Royce 80
Romans 3, 4
Rose 69
Rothay 33, 34, 37, 44, 55
Rothay, river 11
Round House – see Belle Isle
Rutherglen 37, 59
Royal Navy 65
Royal Windermere Yacht Club 59, 63, 71, 93
Royal Naval Air Service 80

St. Mary's Holme 5
St. Vincent, Admiral 18
Satanella 76, 77
Sawrey 47
Schneider, H. W. 52-4, 63, 87
Schollick, Messrs. E. J. 31
Science Museum, London 94
Scott, Sir Walter 17
Seath, T. B. & Co. 37, 38, 44, 52, 59
Segrave, Sir Henry 80, 82
Shamrock 69
Shorts Sunderland 84-6
Sicily 39
Silverholme 16
Sissons, William 71, 76
Sladen, Alfred 63, 64, 66, 67, 71, 73, 74, 94
Sladen, Mortimer 63, 71
Slingsby 84
Southport 87
Staniforth, Rev. Thomas 17, 21, 56, 63
Stephens, R. B. 79
Staveley Meadows 50
Storey, Issac 64
Storrs Hall 5, 16, 17, 20, 25, 31, 36, 56, 63, 69
Storrs Temple 18, 20, 56
Strickland, Agnes 20
Swallow 76, 94
'Swallows & Amazons' 55
Swan I 36, 37, 43, 50, 55
Swan II 44
Swan Hotel 34
Swan Inn 51
Swift 34, 37, 43, 44, 45
Swinburn, Mr. 25, 56
Swines Ness 40

Teal 42, 43
Teal II 44

Tern 37, 44
Thistle 69
Tomlinson, Mr. 79, 89
Town End 16
Troutbeck Bridge 69

Ullswater 90, 92
Ulverston 31, 34
Ulverston Brass Band 13

Vickers Armstrong Ltd. 40
Vickers machine guns 84, 85
Vikings 4

Wagtail 58, 77
Wakefield, E. W. 78, 79
Wakefield, John 15
Wanlass Howe 58
Watercrook 3
Waterhen 38, 78, 79
Waterside Cottage 56
Water Viper 94
Watson, William of Ambleside 9, 11
Westmorland Gazette 39
Westmorland 42
White Hall 20
White of Newby Bridge 9, 25
White, Capt. 28
White, Mr. 51
White Cross Bay 84
William IV 20
Wilberforce, William 21
Williamson, Mr. 77
Wind 69
Windermere Motor Boat Club 79, 80
Windermere Nautical Trust 93, 94
Windermere Iron Steamboat Co. 27, 28, 29, 31
Windermere Sailing Club 56, 59
Windermere Steam Yacht Co. 13, 25, 31, 43
Windermere United Steam Yacht Co. 31, 32, 34, 36, 39, 43
Wordsworth, William 17
Workington 9
Wraith 67
Wray Castle 23, 25, 54, 56, 57, 66
Wray Church 54
Wrynose 3
Wyvern 58
Wyvenhoe 44, 71

Yachts 17 ft. 70, 71
Yachts 20 ft. 56
Yachts 22 ft. 57
Yacht, 1780 56, 87, 94
Yacht, 1745 87

An Accurate MAP of the Grand Lake of WIN
WESTMORLAN